Qt 5 Blueprints

Design, build, and deploy cross-platform GUI projects using the amazingly powerful Qt 5 framework

Symeon Huang

[PACKT] **open source**
PUBLISHING   community experience distilled

BIRMINGHAM - MUMBAI

Qt 5 Blueprints

First published: March 2015

Production reference: 1240315

Published by Packt Publishing Ltd.
Livery Place
35 Livery Street
Birmingham B3 2PB, UK.

ISBN 978-1-78439-461-5

www.packtpub.com

About the Reviewers

Lee Zhi Eng is a 3D artist-turned-programmer who worked as a game artist and programmer in several local game studios in his native country before becoming a contractor and a part-time lecturer at a local university and teaching game development subjects, particularly those related to Unity Engine and Unreal Engine 4. You can find more information about him at http://www.zhieng.com.

Sudhendu Kumar has been a GNU/Linux user for more than 7 years. Currently, he is a software developer for a networking giant, and in his free time, he also contributes to KDE.

> I would like to thank the publishers for giving me the opportunity to review this book. I hope readers find it useful and enjoy reading it and playing around with Qt/Qml applications, not only on desktop devices but also on mobile platforms.

Mickael Minarie is a software developer who graduated from the University of Clermont-Ferrand (bachelor's in embedded systems) and Robert Gordon University, Aberdeen (bachelor's in computer science). He has worked on freelance projects, developing some programs in C++/Qt for embedded systems or in programs linked with photos and videos.

He now lives in France, but he has lived in the UK and Canada for some years.

He is an analog photography and video enthusiast and has written articles for photography fanzines.

www.PacktPub.com

Support files, eBooks, discount offers, and more

For support files and downloads related to your book, please visit www.PacktPub.com.

Did you know that Packt offers eBook versions of every book published, with PDF and ePub files available? You can upgrade to the eBook version at www.PacktPub.com and as a print book customer, you are entitled to a discount on the eBook copy. Get in touch with us at service@packtpub.com for more details.

At www.PacktPub.com, you can also read a collection of free technical articles, sign up for a range of free newsletters and receive exclusive discounts and offers on Packt books and eBooks.

https://www2.packtpub.com/books/subscription/packtlib

Do you need instant solutions to your IT questions? PacktLib is Packt's online digital book library. Here, you can search, access, and read Packt's entire library of books.

Why subscribe?

- Fully searchable across every book published by Packt
- Copy and paste, print, and bookmark content
- On demand and accessible via a web browser

Free access for Packt account holders

If you have an account with Packt at www.PacktPub.com, you can use this to access PacktLib today and view 9 entirely free books. Simply use your login credentials for immediate access.

Table of Contents

Preface

Qt has been developed as a cross-platform framework and has been provided free to the public for years. It's mainly used to build GUI applications. It also provides thousands of APIs for easier development.

Qt 5, the latest major version of Qt, has once again proven to be the most popular cross-platform toolkit. With all these platform-independent classes and functions, you only need to code once, and then you can make it run everywhere.

In addition to the traditional and powerful C++, Qt Quick 2, which is more mature, can help web developers to develop dynamic and reliable applications, since QML is very similar to JavaScript.

What this book covers

Chapter 1, *Creating Your First Qt Application*, takes you through the fundamental concepts of Qt, such as signals and slots, and helps you create your first Qt and Qt Quick applications.

Chapter 2, *Building a Beautiful Cross-platform Clock*, teaches you how to read and write configurations and handle cross-platform development.

Chapter 3, *Cooking an RSS Reader with Qt Quick*, demonstrates how to develop a stylish RSS Reader in QML, which is a script language quite similar to JavaScript.

Chapter 4, *Controlling Camera and Taking Photos*, shows you how to access camera devices through the Qt APIs and make use of the status and menu bars.

Chapter 5, *Extending Paint Applications with Plugins*, teaches you how to make applications extendable and write plugins, by using the Paint application as as an example.

Chapter 6, Getting Wired and Managing Downloads, shows you how to utilize Qt's network module using the progress bar, as well as learning about threaded programming in Qt.

Chapter 7, Parsing JSON and XML Documents to Use Online APIs, teaches you how to parse JSON and XML documents in both Qt/C++ and Qt Quick/QML, which is essential to obtain data from online APIs.

Chapter 8, Enabling Your Qt Application to Support Other Languages, demonstrates how to make internationalized applications, translate strings using Qt Linguist, and then load translation files dynamically.

Chapter 9, Deploying Applications on Other Devices, shows you how to package and make your applications redistributable on Windows, Linux, and Android.

Chapter 10, Don't Panic When You Encounter These Issues, gives you some solutions and advice for common issues during Qt and Qt Quick application development and shows you how to debug Qt and Qt Quick applications.

What you need for this book

Qt is cross-platform, which means you can use it on almost all operating systems, including Windows, Linux, BSD, and Mac OS X. The hardware requirements are listed as follows:

- A computer (PC or Macintosh)
- A webcam or a connected camera device
- Available Internet connection

An Android phone or tablet is not required, but is recommended so that you can test applications on a real Android device.

All the software mentioned in this book, including Qt itself, is free of charge and can be downloaded from the Internet.

Who this book is for

If you are a programmer looking for a truly cross-platform GUI framework to help you save time by side-stepping issues involving incompatibility between different platforms and building applications using Qt 5 for multiple targets, this book is most certainly intended for you. It is assumed that you have basic programming experience of C++.

Conventions

In this book, you will find a number of text styles that distinguish between different kinds of information. Here are some examples of these styles and an explanation of their meaning.

Code words in text, database table names, folder names, filenames, file extensions, pathnames, dummy URLs, user input, and Twitter handles are shown as follows: "The UI files are under the `Forms` directory."

A block of code is set as follows:

```cpp
#include "mainwindow.h"
#include <QApplication>

int main(int argc, char *argv[])
{
    QApplication a(argc, argv);
    MainWindow w;
    w.show();

    return a.exec();
}
```

When we wish to draw your attention to a particular part of a code block, the relevant lines or items are set in bold:

```cpp
#include <QStyleOption>
#include <QPainter>
#include <QPaintEvent>
#include <QMouseEvent>
#include <QResizeEvent>
#include "canvas.h"

Canvas::Canvas(QWidget *parent) :
  QWidget(parent)
{
}

void Canvas::paintEvent(QPaintEvent *e)
{
  QPainter painter(this);

  QStyleOption opt;
  opt.initFrom(this);
```

```cpp
  this->style()->drawPrimitive(QStyle::PE_Widget, &opt, &painter,
    this);

  painter.drawImage(e->rect().topLeft(), image);
}

void Canvas::updateImage()
{
  QPainter painter(&image);
  painter.setPen(QColor(Qt::black));
  painter.setRenderHint(QPainter::Antialiasing);
  painter.drawPolyline(m_points.data(), m_points.count());
  this->update();
}

void Canvas::mousePressEvent(QMouseEvent *e)
{
  m_points.clear();
  m_points.append(e->localPos());
  updateImage();
}

void Canvas::mouseMoveEvent(QMouseEvent *e)
{
  m_points.append(e->localPos());
  updateImage();
}

void Canvas::mouseReleaseEvent(QMouseEvent *e)
{
  m_points.append(e->localPos());
  updateImage();
}

void Canvas::resizeEvent(QResizeEvent *e)
{
  QImage newImage(e->size(), QImage::Format_RGB32);
  newImage.fill(Qt::white);
  QPainter painter(&newImage);
  painter.drawImage(0, 0, image);
  image = newImage;
  QWidget::resizeEvent(e);
}
```

Any command-line input or output is written as follows:

```
..\..\bin\binarycreator.exe -c config\config.xml -p packages
internationalization_installer.exe
```

New terms and **important words** are shown in bold. Words that you see on the screen, for example, in menus or dialog boxes, appear in the text like this: " Navigate to **File** | **New File** or **Project**."

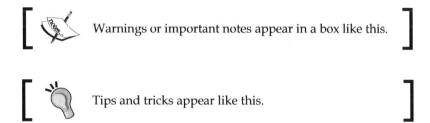

Warnings or important notes appear in a box like this.

Tips and tricks appear like this.

Reader feedback

Feedback from our readers is always welcome. Let us know what you think about this book—what you liked or disliked. Reader feedback is important for us as it helps us develop titles that you will really get the most out of.

To send us general feedback, simply e-mail feedback@packtpub.com, and mention the book's title in the subject of your message.

If there is a topic that you have expertise in and you are interested in either writing or contributing to a book, see our author guide at www.packtpub.com/authors.

Customer support

Now that you are the proud owner of a Packt book, we have a number of things to help you to get the most from your purchase.

Downloading the example code

You can download the example code files from your account at http://www.packtpub.com for all the Packt Publishing books you have purchased. If you purchased this book elsewhere, you can visit http://www.packtpub.com/support and register to have the files e-mailed directly to you.

Errata

Although we have taken every care to ensure the accuracy of our content, mistakes do happen. If you find a mistake in one of our books—maybe a mistake in the text or the code—we would be grateful if you could report this to us. By doing so, you can save other readers from frustration and help us improve subsequent versions of this book. If you find any errata, please report them by visiting http://www.packtpub.com/submit-errata, selecting your book, clicking on the **Errata Submission Form** link, and entering the details of your errata. Once your errata are verified, your submission will be accepted and the errata will be uploaded to our website or added to any list of existing errata under the Errata section of that title.

To view the previously submitted errata, go to https://www.packtpub.com/books/content/support and enter the name of the book in the search field. The required information will appear under the **Errata** section.

Piracy

Piracy of copyrighted material on the Internet is an ongoing problem across all media. At Packt, we take the protection of our copyright and licenses very seriously. If you come across any illegal copies of our works in any form on the Internet, please provide us with the location address or website name immediately so that we can pursue a remedy.

Please contact us at copyright@packtpub.com with a link to the suspected pirated material.

We appreciate your help in protecting our authors and our ability to bring you valuable content.

Questions

If you have a problem with any aspect of this book, you can contact us at questions@packtpub.com, and we will do our best to address the problem.

1
Creating Your First Qt Application

GUI programming is not as difficult as you think. At least it's not when you come to the world of Qt. This book will take you through this world and give you an insight into this incredibly amazing toolkit. It doesn't matter whether you've heard of it or not, as long as you have essential knowledge of C++ programming.

In this chapter, we will get you comfortable with the development of Qt applications. Simple applications are used as a demonstration for you to cover the following topics:

- Creating a new project
- Changing the layout of widgets
- Understanding the mechanism of signals and slots
- Connecting two signals
- Creating a Qt Quick application
- Connecting C++ slots to QML signals

Creating a new project

If you haven't installed Qt 5, refer to `http://www.qt.io/download` to install the latest version of it. It's recommended that you install the Community version, which is totally free and compliant with GPL/LGPL. Typically, the installer will install both **Qt Library** and **Qt Creator** for you. In this book, we will use Qt 5.4.0 and Qt Creator 3.3.0. Later versions may have slight differences but the concept remains the same. It's highly recommended that you install Qt Creator if you don't have it on your computer, because all the tutorials in this book are based on it. It is also the official IDE for the development of Qt applications. Although you may be able to develop Qt applications with other IDEs, it tends to be much more complex. So if you're ready, let's go for it by performing the following steps:

1. Open Qt Creator.
2. Navigate to **File** | **New File** or **Project**.
3. Select **Qt Widgets Application**.
4. Enter the project's name and location. In this case, the project's name is `layout_demo`.

You may wish to follow the wizard and keep the default values. After this process, Qt Creator will generate the skeleton of the project based on your choices. The UI files are under the `Forms` directory. When you double-click on a UI file, Qt Creator will redirect you to the integrated designer. The mode selector should have **Design** highlighted, and the main window should contain several sub-windows to let you design the user interface. This is exactly what we are going to do. For more details about Qt Creator UI, refer to `http://doc.qt.io/qtcreator/creator-quick-tour.html`.

Drag three push buttons from the widget box (widget palette) into the frame of **MainWindow** in the center. The default text displayed on these buttons is **PushButton**, but you can change the text if you want by double-clicking on the button. In this case, I changed the buttons to `Hello`, `Hola`, and `Bonjour`, accordingly. Note that this operation won't affect the `objectName` property. In order to keep it neat and easy to find, we need to change the `objectName` property. The right-hand side of the UI contains two windows. The upper-right section includes **Object Inspector** and the lower-right side includes **Property Editor**. Just select a push button; you can easily change `objectName` in **Property Editor**. For the sake of convenience, I changed these buttons' `objectName` properties to `helloButton`, `holaButton`, and `bonjourButton` respectively.

It's a good habit to use lowercase for the first letter of objectName and an uppercase letter for **Class name**. This helps your code to be more readable by people who are familiar with this convention.

Okay, it's time to see what you have done to the user interface of your first Qt application. Click on **Run** on the left-hand side panel. It will build the project automatically and then run it. It's amazing to see that the application has the exact same interface as the design, isn't it? If everything is alright, the application should appear similar to what is shown in the following screenshot:

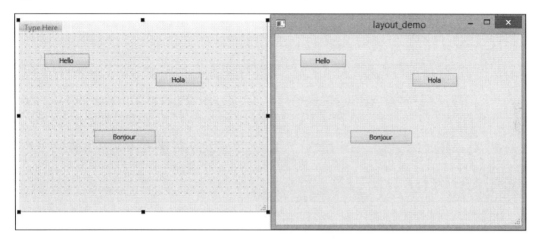

You may want to look at the source code and see what happened there. So, let's go back to the source code by returning to the **Edit** mode. Click on the **Edit** button in the mode selector. Then, double-click on main.cpp in the Sources folder of the **Projects** tree view. The code for main.cpp is shown as follows:

```
#include "mainwindow.h"
#include <QApplication>

int main(int argc, char *argv[])
{
    QApplication a(argc, argv);
    MainWindow w;
    w.show();

    return a.exec();
}
```

The QApplication class manages the GUI application's control flow and the main settings.

Actually, you don't need to and you probably won't change too much in this file. The first line of the main scope just initializes the applications on a user's desktop and handles some events. Then there is also an object, w, which belongs to the MainWindow class. As for the last line, it ensures that the application won't terminate after execution but will keep in an event loop, so that it is able to respond to external events such as mouse clicks and window state changes.

Last but not least, let's see what happens during the initialization of the MainWindow object, w. It is the content of mainwindow.h, shown as follows:

```
#ifndef MAINWINDOW_H
#define MAINWINDOW_H

#include <QMainWindow>

namespace Ui {
    class MainWindow;
}

class MainWindow : public QMainWindow
{
    Q_OBJECT

public:
    explicit MainWindow(QWidget *parent = 0);
    ~MainWindow();

private:
    Ui::MainWindow *ui;
};

#endif // MAINWINDOW_H
```

You may feel a bit surprised seeing a Q_OBJECT macro if this is your first time writing a Qt application. In the QObject documentation, it says:

The Q_OBJECT macro must appear in the private section of a class definition that declares its own signals and slots or that uses other services provided by Qt's meta-object system.

Well, this means that QObject has to be declared if you're going to use Qt's meta-object system and (or) its signals and slots mechanism. The signals and slots, which are almost the core of Qt, will be included later in this chapter.

There is a private member named ui, which is a pointer of the MainWindow class of the Ui namespace. Do you remember the UI file we edited before? What the magic of Qt does is that it links the UI file and the parental source code. We can manipulate the UI through code lines as well as design it in Qt Creator's integrated designer. Finally, let's look into the construction function of MainWindow in mainwindow.cpp:

```
#include "mainwindow.h"
#include "ui_mainwindow.h"

MainWindow::MainWindow(QWidget *parent) :
    QMainWindow(parent),
    ui(new Ui::MainWindow)
{
    ui->setupUi(this);
}

MainWindow::~MainWindow()
{
    delete ui;
}
```

Did you see where the user interface comes from? It's the member setupUi function of Ui::MainWindow that initializes it and sets it up for us. You may want to check what happens if we change the member function to something like this:

```
MainWindow::MainWindow(QWidget *parent) :
    QMainWindow(parent),
    ui(new Ui::MainWindow)
{
    ui->setupUi(this);
    ui->holaButton->setEnabled(false);
}
```

What happened here? The Hola button can't be clicked on because we disabled it! It has the same effect if the **enabled** box is unchecked in the designer instead of writing a statement here. Please apply this change before heading to the next topic, because we don't need a disabled push button to do any demonstrations in this chapter.

Changing the layout of widgets

You already know how to add and move widgets in the **Design** mode. Now, we need to make the UI neat and tidy. I'll show you how to do this step by step.

A quick way to delete a widget is to select it and press the **Delete** button. Meanwhile, some widgets, such as the menu bar, status bar, and toolbar can't be selected, so we have to right-click on them in **Object Inspector** and delete them. Since they are useless in this example, it's safe to remove them and we can do this for good.

Okay, let's understand what needs to be done after the removal. You may want to keep all these push buttons on the same horizontal axis. To do this, perform the following steps:

1. Select all the push buttons either by clicking on them one by one while keeping the *Ctrl* key pressed or just drawing an enclosing rectangle containing all the buttons.

2. Right-click and select **Layout | LayOut Horizontally**, The keyboard shortcut for this is *Ctrl + H*.

3. Resize the horizontal layout and adjust its `layoutSpacing` by selecting it and dragging any of the points around the selection box until it fits best.

Hmm…! You may have noticed that the text of the **Bonjour** button is longer than the other two buttons, and it should be wider than the others. How do you do this? You can change the property of the horizontal layout object's `layoutStretch` property in **Property Editor**. This value indicates the stretch factors of the widgets inside the horizontal layout. They would be laid out in proportion. Change it to 3,3,4, and there you are. The stretched size definitely won't be smaller than the minimum size hint. This is how the zero factor works when there is a nonzero natural number, which means that you need to keep the minimum size instead of getting an error with a zero divisor.

Now, drag **Plain Text Edit** just below, and not inside, the horizontal layout. Obviously, it would be neater if we could extend the plain text edit's width. However, we don't have to do this manually. In fact, we could change the layout of the parent, **MainWindow**. That's it! Right-click on **MainWindow**, and then navigate to **Lay out | Lay Out Vertically**. Wow! All the children widgets are automatically extended to the inner boundary of **MainWindow**; they are kept in a vertical order. You'll also find **Layout** settings in the `centralWidget` property, which is exactly the same thing as the previous horizontal layout.

The last thing to make this application halfway decent is to change the title of the window. MainWindow is not the title you want, right? Click on **MainWindow** in the object tree. Then, scroll down its properties to find **windowTitle**. Name it whatever you want. In this example, I changed it to Greeting. Now, run the application again and you will see it looks like what is shown in the following screenshot:

Understanding the mechanism of signals and slots

It is really important to keep your curiosity and to explore what on earth these properties do. However, please remember to revert the changes you made to the app, as we are about to enter the core part of Qt, that is, signals and slots.

Signals and slots are used for communication between objects. The signals and slots mechanism is a central feature of Qt and probably the part that differs the most from the features provided by other frameworks.

Have you ever wondered why a window closes after the **Close** button is clicked on? Developers who are familiar with other toolkits would say that the **Close** button being clicked on is an event, and this event is bound with a callback function that is responsible for closing the window. Well, it's not quite the same in the world of Qt. Since Qt uses a mechanism called signals and slots, it makes the callback function weakly coupled to the event. Also, we usually use the terms signal and slot in Qt. A signal is emitted when a particular event occurs. A slot is a function that is called in response to a particular signal. The following simple and schematic diagram helps you understand the relation between signals, events, and slots:

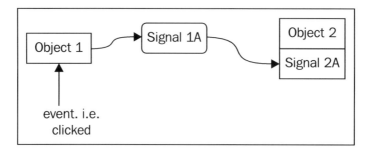

Qt has tons of predefined signals and slots, which cover its general purposes. However, it's indeed commonplace to add your own slots to handle the target signals. You may also be interested in subclassing widgets and writing your own signals, which will be covered later. The mechanism of signals and slots was designed to be type-safe because of its requirement of the list of the same arguments. In fact, the slot may have a shorter arguments list than the signal since it can ignore the extras. You can have as many arguments as you want. This enables you to forget about the wildcard `void*` type in C and other toolkits.

Since Qt 5, this mechanism is even safer because we can use a new syntax of signals and slots to deal with the connections. A conversion of a piece of code is demonstrated here. Let's see what a typical connect statement in old style is:

```
connect(sender, SIGNAL(textChanged(QString)), receiver,
    SLOT(updateText(QString)));
```

This can be rewritten in a new syntax style:

```
connect(sender, &Sender::textChanged, receiver,
    &Receiver::updateText);
```

In the traditional way of writing code, the verification of signals and slots only happens at runtime. In the new style, the compiler can detect the mismatches in the types of arguments and the existence of signals and slots at compile time.

As long as it is possible, all connect statements are written in the new syntax style in this book.

Now, let's get back to our application. I'll show you how to display some words in a plain text edit when the **Hello** button is clicked on. First of all, we need to create a slot since Qt has already predefined the clicked signal for the QPushButton class. Edit mainwindow.h and add a slot declaration:

```
#ifndef MAINWINDOW_H
#define MAINWINDOW_H

#include <QMainWindow>

namespace Ui {
    class MainWindow;
}

class MainWindow : public QMainWindow
{
    Q_OBJECT

public:
    explicit MainWindow(QWidget *parent = 0);
    ~MainWindow();

private slots:
    void displayHello();

private:
    Ui::MainWindow *ui;
};

#endif // MAINWINDOW_H
```

As you can see, it's the slots keyword that distinguishes slots from ordinary functions. I declared it private to restrict access permission. You have to declare it a public slot if you need to invoke it in an object from other classes. After this declaration, we have to implement it in the mainwindow.cpp file. The implementation of the displayHello slot is written as follows:

```
void MainWindow::displayHello()
{
    ui->plainTextEdit->appendPlainText(QString("Hello"));
}
```

It simply calls a member function of the plain text edit in order to add a `Hello` QString to it. `QString` is a core class that Qt has introduced. It provides a Unicode character string, which efficiently solves the internationalization issue. It's also convenient to convert a `QString` class to `std::string` and vice versa. Besides, just like the other `QObject` classes, `QString` uses an implicit sharing mechanism to reduce memory usage and avoid needless copying. If you don't want to get concerned about the scenes shown in the following code, just take `QString` as an improved version of `std::string`. Now, we need to connect this slot to the signal that the **Hello** push button will emit:

```
MainWindow::MainWindow(QWidget *parent)  :
    QMainWindow(parent),
    ui(new Ui::MainWindow)
{
    ui->setupUi(this);

    connect(ui->helloButton, &QPushButton::clicked, this,
        &MainWindow::displayHello);
}
```

What I did is add a `connect` statement to the constructor of `MainWindow`. In fact, we can connect signals and slots anywhere and at any time. However, the connection only exists after this line gets executed. So, it's a common practice to have lots of `connect` statements in the construction functions instead of spreading them out. For a better understanding, run your application and see what happens when you click on the **Hello** button. Every time you click, a **Hello** text will be appended to the plain text edit. The following screenshot is what happened after we clicked on the **Hello** button three times:

Getting confused? Let me walk you through this. When you clicked on the **Hello** button, it emitted a clicked signal. Then, the code inside the displayHello slot got executed, because we connected the clicked signal of the **Hello** button to the displayHello slot of MainWindow. What the displayHello slot did is that it simply appended Hello to the plain text edit.

It may take you some time to fully understand the mechanism of signals and slots. Just take your time. I'll show you another example of how to disconnect such a connection after we clicked on the **Hola** button. Similarly, add a declaration of the slot to the header file and define it in the source file. I pasted the content of the mainwindow.h header file, as follows:

```
#ifndef MAINWINDOW_H
#define MAINWINDOW_H

#include <QMainWindow>

namespace Ui {
    class MainWindow;
}

class MainWindow : public QMainWindow
{
    Q_OBJECT

public:
    explicit MainWindow(QWidget *parent = 0);
    ~MainWindow();

private slots:
    void displayHello();
    void onHolaClicked();

private:
    Ui::MainWindow *ui;
};

#endif // MAINWINDOW_H
```

It's only declaring a onHolaClicked slot that differed from the original. Here's the content of the source file:

```
#include "mainwindow.h"
#include "ui_mainwindow.h"
```

```
MainWindow::MainWindow(QWidget *parent) :
    QMainWindow(parent),
    ui(new Ui::MainWindow)
{

    ui->setupUi(this);

    connect(ui->helloButton, &QPushButton::clicked, this,
        &MainWindow::displayHello);
    connect(ui->holaButton, &QPushButton::clicked, this,
        &MainWindow::onHolaClicked);
}

MainWindow::~MainWindow()
{

    delete ui;
}

void MainWindow::displayHello()
{
    ui->plainTextEdit->appendPlainText(QString("Hello"));
}

void MainWindow::onHolaClicked()
{
    ui->plainTextEdit->appendPlainText(QString("Hola"));
    disconnect(ui->helloButton, &QPushButton::clicked, this,
        &MainWindow::displayHello);
}
```

You'll find that the **Hello** button no longer works after you clicked on the **Hola** button. This is because in the onHolaClicked slot, we just disconnected the binding between the clicked signal of helloButton and the displayHello slot of MainWindow. Actually, disconnect has some overloaded functions and can be used in a more destructive way. For example, you may want to disconnect all connections between a specific signal sender and a specific receiver:

```
disconnect(ui->helloButton, 0, this, 0);
```

If you want to disconnect all the slots associated with a signal, since a signal can be connected to as many slots as you wish, the code can be written like this:

```
disconnect(ui->helloButton, &QPushButton::clicked, 0, 0);
```

We can also disconnect all the signals in an object, whatever slots they might be connected to. The following code will disconnect all the signals in `helloButton`, which of course includes the clicked signal:

```
disconnect(ui->helloButton, 0, 0, 0);
```

Just like a signal, a slot can be connected to as many signals as you want. However, there's no such function to disconnect a specific slot from all the signals.

 Always remember the signals and slots that you have connected.

Apart from the new syntax for traditional connections of signals and slots, Qt 5 has offered a new way to simplify such a binding process with C++11 lambda expressions. As you may have noticed, it's kind of tedious to declare a slot in the header file, define it in the source code file, and then connect it to a signal. It's worthwhile if the slot has a lot of statements, otherwise it becomes time consuming and increases the complexity. Before we go any further, we need to turn on C++11 support on Qt. Edit the pro file (`layout_demo.pro` in my example) and add the following line to it:

```
CONFIG += c++11
```

 Note that some old compilers don't support C++11. If this happens, upgrade your compiler.

Now, you need to navigate to **Build | Run qmake** to reconfigure the project properly. If everything is okay, we can go back to editing the `mainwindow.cpp` file. This way, there is no need to declare a slot and define and connect it. Just add a `connect` statement to the construction function of `MainWindow`:

```
connect(ui->bonjourButton, &QPushButton::clicked, [this](){
    ui->plainTextEdit->appendPlainText(QString("Bonjour"));
});
```

It's very straightforward, isn't it? The third argument is a lambda expression, which was added to C++ since C++11.

 For more details about lambda expression, visit `http://en.cppreference.com/w/cpp/language/lambda`.

This pair of signal and slot connection is done if you don't do need to to disconnect such a connection. However, if you need, you have to save this connection, which is a QMetaObject::Connection type. In order to disconnect this connection elsewhere, it would be better to declare it as a variable of MainWindow. So the header file becomes as follows:

```
#ifndef MAINWINDOW_H
#define MAINWINDOW_H

#include <QMainWindow>

namespace Ui {
    class MainWindow;
}

class MainWindow : public QMainWindow
{
    Q_OBJECT

public:
    explicit MainWindow(QWidget *parent = 0);
    ~MainWindow();

private slots:
    void displayHello();
    void onHolaClicked();

private:
    Ui::MainWindow *ui;
    QMetaObject::Connection bonjourConnection;
};

#endif // MAINWINDOW_H
```

Here, I declared bonjourConnection as an object of QMetaObject::Connection so that we can save the connection dealing with an unnamed slot. Similarly, the disconnection happens in onHolaClicked, so there won't be any new Bonjour text on screen after we click on the **Hola** button. Here is the content of mainwindow.cpp:

```
#include "mainwindow.h"
#include "ui_mainwindow.h"

MainWindow::MainWindow(QWidget *parent) :
    QMainWindow(parent),
```

```
    ui (new Ui::MainWindow)
{
    ui->setupUi(this);

    connect(ui->helloButton, &QPushButton::clicked, this,
        &MainWindow::displayHello);
    connect(ui->holaButton, &QPushButton::clicked, this,
        &MainWindow::onHolaClicked);
    bonjourConnection = connect(ui->bonjourButton,
        &QPushButton::clicked, [this](){
        ui->plainTextEdit->appendPlainText(QString("Bonjour"));
    });
}

MainWindow::~MainWindow()
{
    delete ui;
}

void MainWindow::displayHello()
{
    ui->plainTextEdit->appendPlainText(QString("Hello"));
}

void MainWindow::onHolaClicked()
{
    ui->plainTextEdit->appendPlainText(QString("Hola"));
    disconnect(ui->helloButton, &QPushButton::clicked, this,
        &MainWindow::displayHello);
    disconnect(bonjourConnection);
}
```

This is indeed another new usage of `disconnect`. It takes in a
`QMetaObject::Connection` object as the only argument. You'll thank this new
overloaded function if you're going to use the lambda expression as a slot.

Connecting two signals

Due to the weak couplings of the Qt signals and slot mechanisms, it is viable to bind signals to each other. It may sound confusing, so let me draw a diagram to make it clear:

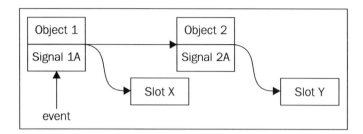

When an event triggers a specific signal, this emitted signal could be another event, which will emit another specific signal. It is not a very common practice, but it tends to be useful when you deal with some complex signals and slot connection networks, especially when tons of events lead to the emission of only a few signals. Although it definitely increases the complexity of the project, binding these signals could simplify the code a lot. Append the following statement to the construction function of `MainWindow`:

```
connect(ui->bonjourButton, &QPushButton::clicked, ui->helloButton,
    &QPushButton::clicked);
```

You'll get two lines in a plain text edit after you click on the **Bonjour** button. The first line is **Bonjour** and the second one is **Hello**. Apparently, this is because we coupled the clicked signal of the **Bonjour** button with the clicked signal of the **Hello** button. The clicked signal of the latter has already been coupled with a slot, which results in the new text line, **Hello**. In fact, it has the same effect as the following statement:

```
connect(ui->bonjourButton, &QPushButton::clicked, [this](){
    emit ui->helloButton->clicked();
});
```

Basically, connecting two signals is a simplified version of connecting a signal and a slot, while the slot is meant to emit another signal. As for priority, the slot(s) of the latter signal will be handled when the event loop is returned to the object.

However, it is impossible to connect two slots because the mechanism requires a signal while a slot is considered a receiver instead of a sender. Therefore, if you want to simplify the connection, just wrap these slots as one slot, which can be used for connections.

Creating a Qt Quick application

We already covered how to create a Qt (C++) application. How about giving the newly introduced Qt Quick application development a try? Qt Quick was introduced in Qt 4.8 and it is now becoming mature in Qt 5. Because the QML file is usually platform-independent, it enables you to develop an application for multiple targets, including mobile operating systems with the same code.

In this chapter, I'll show you how to create a simple Qt Quick application based on Qt Quick Controls 1.2, as follows:

1. Create a new project named `HelloQML`.

2. Select **Qt Quick Application** instead of **Qt Widgets Application**, which we chose previously.

3. Select **Qt Quick Controls 1.2** when the wizard navigates you to **Select Qt Quick Components Set**.

Qt Quick Controls has been introduced since Qt 5.1 and is highly recommended because it enables you to build a complete and native user interface. You can also control the top-level window properties from QML. Getting confused by QML and Qt Quick?

QML is a user interface specification and programming language. It allows developers and designers alike to create highly performant, fluidly animated, and visually appealing applications. QML offers a highly readable, declarative, JSON-like syntax with support for imperative JavaScript expressions combined with dynamic property bindings.

While Qt Quick is the standard library for QML, it sounds like the relation between STL and C++. The difference is that QML is dedicated to user interface design and Qt Quick includes a lot of visual types, animations, and so on. Before we go any further, I want to inform you that QML is different from C++ but similar to JavaScript and JSON.

Edit the `main.qml` file under the root of the `Resources` file, `qml.qrc`, which Qt Creator has generated for our new Qt Quick project. Let's see how the code should be:

```
import QtQuick 2.3
import QtQuick.Controls 1.2
```

```
ApplicationWindow {
    visible: true
    width: 640
    height: 480
    title: qsTr("Hello QML")

    menuBar: MenuBar {
        Menu {
            title: qsTr("File")
            MenuItem {
                text: qsTr("Exit")
                shortcut: "Ctrl+Q"
                onTriggered: Qt.quit()
            }
        }
    }

    Text {
        id: hw
        text: qsTr("Hello World")
        font.capitalization: Font.AllUppercase
        anchors.centerIn: parent
    }

    Label {
        anchors { bottom: hw.top; bottomMargin: 5;
            horizontalCenter: hw.horizontalCenter }
        text: qsTr("Hello Qt Quick")
    }
}
```

If you have ever touched Java or Python, the first two lines won't be too unfamiliar to you. It simply imports Qt Quick and Qt Quick Controls, and the number following is the version of the library. You may need to change the version if there is a newer library. Importing other libraries is a common practice when developing Qt Quick applications.

The body of this QML source file is actually in the JSON style, which enables you to understand the hierarchy of the user interface through the code. Here, the root item is ApplicationWindow, which is basically the same thing as MainWindow in the previous topics, and we use braces to enclose the statements just like in a JSON file. Although you could use a semicolon to mark an ending of a statement just like we do in C++, there is no need to do this. As you can see, the property definition needs a colon if it's a single-line statement and enclosing braces if it contains more than one subproperty.

The statements are kind of self explanatory and they are similar to the properties that we saw in the Qt Widgets application. A `qsTr` function is used for internationalization and localization. Strings marked by `qsTr` could be translated by Qt Linguist. In addition to this, you don't need to care about QString and `std::string` any more. All the strings in QML are encoded in the same coding as the QML file and the QML file is created in UTF-8 by default.

As for the signals and slots mechanism in Qt Quick, it's easy if you only use QML to write the callback function to the corresponding slot. Here, we execute `Qt.quit()` inside the `onTriggered` slot of `MenuItem`. It's viable to connect the signal of a QML item to a C++ object's slot, which I'll introduce later.

When you run this application in Windows, you can barely find the difference between the `Text` item and the `Label` item. However, on some platforms, or when you change the system font and/or its color, you'll find that `Label` follows the font and the color scheme of the system, while `Text` doesn't. Although you can use the properties of `Text` to customize the appearance of `Label`, it would be better to use the system settings to keep the looks of the application native. Well, if you run this application right now, it will appear similar to what is shown in the following screenshot:

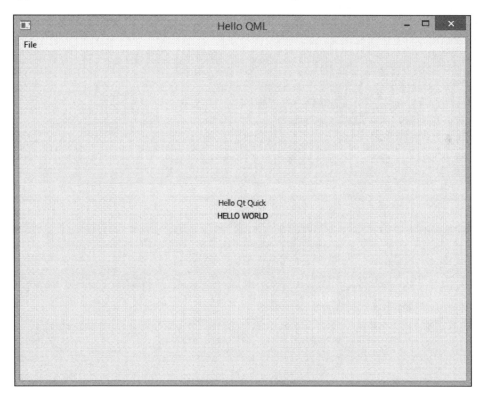

Because there is no separate UI file for the Qt Quick applications, only a QML file, we use the `anchors` property to position the items, and `anchors.centerIn` will position the item in the center of the parent. There is an integrated Qt Quick Designer in Qt Creator, which could help you design the user interface of a Qt Quick application. If you need it, just navigate to **Design** mode when you're editing a QML file. However, I suggest you stay in **Edit** mode to understand the meaning of each statement.

Connecting C++ slots to QML signals

The separation of the user interface and backend allows us to connect C++ slots to the QML signals. Although it's possible to write processing functions in QML and manipulate interface items in C++, it violates the principle of the separation. Therefore, you may want to know how to connect a C++ slot to a QML signal at first. As for connecting a QML slot to a C++ signal, I'll introduce that later in this book.

In order to demonstrate this, we need to create a C++ class in the first place by right-clicking on the project in the **Projects** panel and selecting **Add New...**. Then, click on **C++ Class** in the pop-up window. The newly created class should at least inherit from `QObject` by choosing `QObject` as its base class. This is because a plain C++ class can't include Qt's slots or signals. The header file's content is displayed as follows:

```cpp
#ifndef PROCESSOR_H
#define PROCESSOR_H

#include <QObject>

class Processor : public QObject
{
    Q_OBJECT
public:
    explicit Processor(QObject *parent = 0);

public slots:
    void onMenuClicked(const QString &);
};

#endif // PROCESSOR_H
```

Here's the content of the source file:

```cpp
#include <QDebug>
#include "processor.h"

Processor::Processor(QObject *parent) :
    QObject(parent)
{
}

void Processor::onMenuClicked(const QString &str)
{
    qDebug() << str;
}
```

The C++ file is the same as the one we dealt with in the previous topics. The onMenuClicked slot I defined is simply to output the string that passes through the signal. Note that you have to include QDebug if you want to use the built-in functions of qDebug, qWarning, qCritical, and so on.

The slot is prepared, so we need to add a signal to the QML file. The QML file is changed to the following code:

```qml
import QtQuick 2.3
import QtQuick.Controls 1.2

ApplicationWindow {
    id: window
    visible: true
    width: 640
    height: 480
    title: qsTr("Hello QML")
    signal menuClicked(string str)

    menuBar: MenuBar {
        Menu {
            title: qsTr("File")
            MenuItem {
                text: qsTr("Exit")
                shortcut: "Ctrl+Q"
                onTriggered: Qt.quit()
            }
            MenuItem {
                text: qsTr("Click Me")
```

```
                    onTriggered: window.menuClicked(text)
                }
            }
        }

    Text {
        id: hw
        text: qsTr("Hello World")
        font.capitalization: Font.AllUppercase
        anchors.centerIn: parent
    }

    Label {
        anchors { bottom: hw.top; bottomMargin: 5;
            horizontalCenter: hw.horizontalCenter }
        text: qsTr("Hello Qt Quick")
    }
}
```

As you can see, I specified the ID of the root ApplicationWindow item to window and declared a signal named menuClicked. In addition to this, there is another MenuItem in the menu file. It emits the menuClicked signal of window, using its text as the parameter.

Now, let's connect the slot in the C++ file to this newly created QML signal. Edit the main.cpp file.

```cpp
#include <QApplication>
#include <QQmlApplicationEngine>
#include "processor.h"

int main(int argc, char *argv[])
{
    QApplication app(argc, argv);

    QQmlApplicationEngine engine;
    engine.load(QUrl(QStringLiteral("qrc:///main.qml")));

    QObject *firstRootItem = engine.rootObjects().first();
    Processor myProcessor;
    QObject::connect(firstRootItem, SIGNAL(menuClicked(QString)),
        &myProcessor, SLOT(onMenuClicked(QString)));

    return app.exec();
}
```

The item in the QML file is accessed as QObject in C++ and it could be cast to QQuickItem. For now, we only need to connect its signal, so QObject will do.

You may notice that I used the old-style syntax of the connect statement. This is because QML is dynamic and the C++ compiler can't detect the existence of the signal in the QML file. Since things in QML are checked at runtime, it doesn't make sense to use the old syntax here.

When you run this application and navigate to **File | Click Me** in the menu bar, you'll see **Application Output** in Qt Creator:

```
"Click Me"
```

Let's review this process again. Triggering the Click Me menu item resulted in the emission of the window's signal menuClicked. This signal passed the text of MenuItem, which is Click Me, to the slot in C++ class Processor, and the processor myProcessor slot onMenuClicked printed the string to the **Application Output** panel.

Summary

In this chapter, we learned the fundamentals of Qt, which included steps for how to create a Qt application. Then, we had a walk-through of both Qt Widgets and Qt Quick, and how to change the layout. Finally, we rounded off by covering an important concept about the mechanism of signals and slots.

In the next chapter, we will have a chance to put this knowledge into practice and get started on building a real-world, and of course cross-platform, Qt application.

2
Building a Beautiful Cross-platform Clock

In this chapter, you will learn that Qt is a great tool to build cross-platform applications. A Qt/C++ clock example is used as a demonstration here. The topics covered in this chapter, which are listed here, are essential for any real-world applications. These are as follows:

- Creating a basic digital clock
- Tweaking the digital clock
- Saving and restoring settings
- Building on Unix platforms

Creating a basic digital clock

It's time to create a new project, so we will create a Qt Widgets application named `Fancy_Clock`.

 We won't utilize any Qt Quick knowledge in this chapter.

Now, change the window title to `Fancy Clock` or any other name that you like. Then, the main window UI needs to be tailored because the clock is displayed at the top of the desktop. The menu bar, status bar, and toolbar are all removed. After that, we need to drag an **LCD Number** widget into `centralWidget`. Next, change the layout of `MainWindow` to **LayOut Horizontally** in order to autoresize the subwidget. The last thing that needs to be done to the UI file is to change **frameShape** to **NoFrame** under the **QFrame** column in the property of `lcdNumber`. If you've done this right, you'll get a prototype of a digital clock, as shown here:

In order to update the LCD number display repeatedly, we have to make use of the `QTimer` class to set up a timer that emits a signal repetitively. In addition to this, we need to create a slot to receive the signal and to update the LCD number display to the current time. Thus, the `QTime` class is also needed. This is how the header file of `MainWindowmainwindow.h` will look now:

```
#ifndef MAINWINDOW_H
#define MAINWINDOW_H

#include <QMainWindow>

namespace Ui {
   class MainWindow;
}

class MainWindow : public QMainWindow
{
```

```
    Q_OBJECT

public:
    explicit MainWindow(QWidget *parent = 0);
    ~MainWindow();

private:
    Ui::MainWindow *ui;

private slots:
    void updateTime();
};


#endif // MAINWINDOW_H
```

As you can see, the only modification made here is the declaration of a private
updateTime slot. As usual, we're supposed to define this slot in mainwindow.cpp,
whose content is pasted here. Note that we need to include QTimer and QTime.

```
#include <QTimer>
#include <QTime>
#include "mainwindow.h"
#include "ui_mainwindow.h"

MainWindow::MainWindow(QWidget *parent) :
    QMainWindow(parent),
    ui(new Ui::MainWindow)
{
    ui->setupUi(this);

    QTimer *timer = new QTimer(this);
    connect(timer, &QTimer::timeout, this, &MainWindow::updateTime);
    timer->start(1000);

    updateTime();
}

MainWindow::~MainWindow()
{
    delete ui;
}

void MainWindow::updateTime()
{
```

```
QTime currentTime = QTime::currentTime();
QString currentTimeText = currentTime.toString("hh:mm");
if (currentTime.second() % 2 == 0) {
  currentTimeText[2] = ' ';
}
ui->lcdNumber->display(currentTimeText);
}
```

Inside the `updateTime` slot, the `QTime` class is used to deal with the time, that is, the clock. This class can provide accuracy of up to 1 millisecond, if the underlying operating system supports it. However, `QTime` has nothing to do with the time zone or daylight saving time. It is, at least, sufficient for our little clock. The `currentTime()` function is a static public function, which is used to create a `QTime` object that contains the system's local time.

As for the second line of the `updateTime` function, we used the `toString` function provided by `QTime` to convert the time to a string, and then saved it in `currentTimeText`. The arguments that are passed to `toString` are in the format of the time string. The full list of expressions can be obtained from **Qt Reference Documentation**. The colon in the middle of the clock should be flashing, just as in the case of a real digital clock. Hence, we used an `if` statement to control this. The colon will vanish when the second's value is even, and it will reappear when the second's value is odd. Here, inside the `if` block, we used the `[2]` operator to get a modifiable reference of the third character because this is the only way to do direct modifications to a character inside a string. Here, the counting of the `currentTimeText` string starts from `0`. Meanwhile, the `at()` function of `QString` returns a constant character, which you have no right to change. At last, this function will let `lcdNumber` display the time string. Now, let's get back to the constructor of `MainWindow`. After the initialization of the UI, the first thing it does is to create a `QTimer` object. Why can't we use a local variable? The answer to that question is because the local variables will be destroyed after the construction of `MainWindow`. If the timer has gone, there's no way to trigger `updateTime` repetitively. We don't use a member variable because there is no need to perform the declaration work in the header file, since we won't use this timer elsewhere.

The `QTimer` class is used to create a repetitive and single-shot timer. It will emit the `timeout` signal at constant intervals after `start` is called. Here, we create one timer and connect the `timeout` signal to the `updateTime` slot so that `updateTime` is called every second.

There is another important aspect in Qt called **parent-child mechanism**. Although it's not as well-known as signals and slots, it plays a crucial role in the development of the Qt applications. Basically speaking, when we create an QObject child with a parent or explicitly set a parent by calling setParent, the parent will add this QObject child to its list of children. Then, when the parent is deleted, it'll go through its list of children and delete each child. In most cases, especially in the design of a UI, the parent-child relationship is set up implicitly. The parent widget or layout automatically becomes the parent object to its children widgets or layouts. In other cases, we have to explicitly set the parent for a QObject child so that the parent can take over its ownership and manage the release of its memory. Hence, we pass the QObject parent, which is this, a MainWindow class to the constructor of QTimer. This ensures that QTimer will be deleted after MainWindow is deleted. That's why we don't have to explicitly write the delete statements in the destructor.

At the end of the constructor, we need to call updateTime explicitly, which will allow the clock to display the current time. If we don't do this, the application will display a zero for a second until the timeout signal is emitted by timer. Now, run your application; it will be similar to the following screenshot:

Tweaking the digital clock

It's time to make this basic digital clock look more beautiful. Let's add something like a transparent background, which sits on top of the frameless window. Using a transparent background can deliver a fantastic visual effect. While the frameless window hides window decorations, including a border and the title bar, a desktop widget, such as a clock, should be frameless and displayed on top of the desktop.

To make our clock translucent, simply add the following line to the constructor of `MainWindow`:

```
setAttribute(Qt::WA_TranslucentBackground);
```

The effect of the `WA_TranslucentBackground` attribute depends on the composition managers on the X11 platforms.

A widget may have lots of attributes, and this function is used to switch on or switch off a specified attribute. It's turned on by default. You need to pass a false Boolean as the second argument to disable an attribute. The full list of `Qt::WidgetAttribute` can be found in the Qt Reference Documentation.

Now, add the following line to the constructor as well, which will make the clock look frameless and make it stay on top of the desktop:

```
setWindowFlags(Qt::WindowStaysOnTopHint |
    Qt::FramelessWindowHint);
```

Similarly, `Qt::WindowFlags` is used to define the type of widget. It controls the behavior of the widget, rather than of its properties. Thus, two hints are given: one is to stay on top and the other is to be frameless. If you want to preserve old flags while setting new ones, you need to add them to the combination.

```
setWindowFlags(Qt::WindowStaysOnTopHint | Qt::FramelessWindowHint
    | windowFlags());
```

Here, the `windowFlags` function is used to retrieve the window flags. One thing you may be interested to know is that `setWindowFlags` will result in the invisibility of the widget after the `show` function. So, you can either call `setWindowFlags` before the `show` function of the window or widget or call `show` again after `setWindowFlags`.

After the modification to the constructor, this is how the clock is expected to look:

There is a useful trick that you can use to hide the clock from the taskbar. Of course, a clock doesn't need to be displayed among the applications in a taskbar. You should never set a flag such as Qt::Tool or Qt::ToolTip alone to achieve this because this will cause the exit behavior of the application to be abnormal. This trick is even simpler; here is the code of main.cpp:

```
#include "mainwindow.h"
#include <QApplication>

int main(int argc, char *argv[])
{
    QApplication a(argc, argv);

    QWidget wid;
    MainWindow w(&wid);
    w.show();

    return a.exec();
}
```

The preceding code makes our `MainWindow` w object a child of `QWidget` wid. The child widgets won't display on the taskbar because there should be only one top parent widget. Meanwhile, our parent widget, wid, doesn't even show. It's tricky, but it's the only one that does the trick without breaking any other logic.

Well, a new problem has just surfaced. The clock is unable to move and the only way to close it is by stopping it through the Qt Creator's panel or through a keyboard shortcut. This is because we declared it as a frameless window, which led to an inability to control it via a window manager. Since there is no way to interact with it, it's impossible to close it by itself. Hence, the solution to this problem is to write our own functions to move and close the clock.

Closing this application may be more urgent. Let's see how to reimplement some functions to achieve this goal. First, we need to declare a new `showContextMenu` slot to display a context menu and reimplement `mouseReleaseEvent`. The following code shows the content of `mainwindow.h`:

```
#ifndef MAINWINDOW_H
#define MAINWINDOW_H

#include <QMainWindow>

namespace Ui {
  class MainWindow;
}

class MainWindow : public QMainWindow
{
  Q_OBJECT
public:
  explicit MainWindow(QWidget *parent = 0);
  ~MainWindow();

private:
  Ui::MainWindow *ui;

private slots:
  void updateTime();
  void showContextMenu(const QPoint &pos);

protected:
  void mouseReleaseEvent(QMouseEvent *);
};

#endif // MAINWINDOW_H
```

There are two new classes defined in the preceding code: QPoint and QMouseEvent. The QPoint class defines a point in the plane by using integer precision. Relatively, there is another class named QPointF, which provides float precision. Well, the QMouseEvent class inherits QEvent and QInputEvent. It contains some parameters that describe a mouse event. Let's see why we need them in mainwindow.cpp:

```cpp
#include <QTimer>
#include <QTime>
#include <QMouseEvent>
#include <QMenu>
#include <QAction>
#include "mainwindow.h"
#include "ui_mainwindow.h"

MainWindow::MainWindow(QWidget *parent) :
  QMainWindow(parent),
  ui(new Ui::MainWindow)
{
  ui->setupUi(this);

  setAttribute(Qt::WA_TranslucentBackground);
  setWindowFlags(Qt::WindowStaysOnTopHint |
    Qt::FramelessWindowHint | windowFlags());

  connect(this, &MainWindow::customContextMenuRequested, this,
    &MainWindow::showContextMenu);

  QTimer *timer = new QTimer(this);
  connect(timer, &QTimer::timeout, this, &MainWindow::updateTime);
  timer->start(1000);

  updateTime();
}

MainWindow::~MainWindow()
{
  delete ui;
}

void MainWindow::updateTime()
{
  QTime currentTime = QTime::currentTime();
  QString currentTimeText = currentTime.toString("hh:mm");
  if (currentTime.second() % 2 == 0) {
```

```
      currentTimeText[2] = ' ';
  }
  ui->lcdNumber->display(currentTimeText);
}

void MainWindow::showContextMenu(const QPoint &pos)
{
  QMenu contextMenu;
  contextMenu.addAction(QString("Exit"), this, SLOT(close()));
  contextMenu.exec(mapToGlobal(pos));
}

void MainWindow::mouseReleaseEvent(QMouseEvent *e)
{
  if (e->button() == Qt::RightButton) {
    emit customContextMenuRequested(e->pos());
  }
  else {
    QMainWindow::mouseReleaseEvent(e);
  }
}
```

Note that you should include QMouseEvent, QMenu, and QAction in order to utilize these classes. There is a predefined customContextMenuRequested signal, which is coupled with the newly created showContextMenu slot. For the sake of consistency, we will follow the rule that Qt defined, which means that the QPoint argument in customContextMenuRequested should be a local position instead of a global position. That's why we need a mapToGlobal function to translate pos to a global position. As for the QMenu class, it provides a menu widget for a menu bar, context menu, or other pop-up menus. So, we create the contextMenu object, and then add a new action with the Exit text. This is coupled with a close slot of MainWindow. The last statement is used to execute the contextMenu object at the specified global position. In other words, this slot will display a pop-up menu at the given position.

The reimplementation of mouseReleaseEvent is done to check the triggered button of the event. If it's the right button, emit the customContextMenuRequested signal with the local position of the mouse. Otherwise, simply call the default mouseReleaseEvent function of QMainWindow.

Make use of the default member functions of the base class when you reimplement it.

Run the application again; you can quit by right-clicking on it and then selecting
Exit. Now, we should continue the reimplementation to make the clock movable.
This time, we need to rewrite two protected functions: `mousePressEvent` and
`mouseMoveEvent`. Therefore, this is how the header file looks:

```
#ifndef MAINWINDOW_H
#define MAINWINDOW_H

#include <QMainWindow>

namespace Ui {
  class MainWindow;
}

class MainWindow : public QMainWindow
{
  Q_OBJECT

public:
  explicit MainWindow(QWidget *parent = 0);
  ~MainWindow();

private:
  Ui::MainWindow *ui;
  QPoint m_mousePos;

private slots:
  void updateTime();
  void showContextMenu(const QPoint &pos);

protected:
  void mouseReleaseEvent(QMouseEvent *);
  void mousePressEvent(QMouseEvent *);
  void mouseMoveEvent(QMouseEvent *);
};

#endif // MAINWINDOW_H
```

There is also a declaration of a new private member variable in the preceding code, m_mousePos, which is a QPoint object used to store the local position of the mouse. The following code defines mousePressEvent and mouseMoveEvent:

```
void MainWindow::mousePressEvent(QMouseEvent *e)
{
   m_mousePos = e->pos();
}

void MainWindow::mouseMoveEvent(QMouseEvent *e)
{
   this->move(e->globalPos() - m_mousePos);
}
```

It's easier than you thought. When a mouse button is pressed, the local position of the mouse is stored as m_mousePos. When the mouse is moving, we call the move function to move MainWindow to a new position. Because the position passed to move is a global position, we need to use globalPos of the event minus the local position of the mouse. Confused? The m_mousePos variable is the mouse's relative position to the top-left point of the parent widget, which is MainWindow in our case. The move function will move the top-left point of MainWindow to the given global position. While the e->globalPos() function is the global position of the mouse and not MainWindow, we need to subtract the relative position of m_mousePos to translate the mouse's global position to the top-left point position of MainWindow. After all this effort, the clock should look much more satisfying.

Saving and restoring settings

Although the clock can be moved, it won't restore its last position after restarting. In addition to this, we can give users some choices to adjust the clock's appearance, such as the font color. To make it work, we need the QSettings class, which provides platform-independent persistent settings. It needs a company or organization name and the name of an application. A typical QSettings object can be constructed by using this line:

```
QSettings settings("Qt5 Blueprints", "Fancy Clock");
```

Here, Qt5 Blueprints is the organization's name and Fancy Clock is the application's name.

The settings are stored in the system registry on Windows, while they are stored in the XML preferences files on Mac OS X and the INI text files on the other Unix operating systems, such as Linux. However, we do not usually need to be concerned with this, since QSettings provides high-level interfaces to manipulate the settings.

If we're going to read and/or write settings in multiple places, we'd better set the organization and application in QCoreApplication, which is inherited by QApplication. The main.cpp file's content is shown as follows:

```cpp
#include "mainwindow.h"
#include <QApplication>

int main(int argc, char *argv[])
{
    QApplication a(argc, argv);

    a.setOrganizationName(QString("Qt5 Blueprints"));
    a.setApplicationName(QString("Fancy Clock"));

    QWidget wid;
    MainWindow w(&wid);
    w.show();

    return a.exec();
}
```

This enables us to use the default QSettings constructor to access the same settings. In order to save the geometry and state of MainWindow, we need to reimplement closeEvent. First, we need to declare closeEvent to be a protected member function, as follows:

```cpp
void closeEvent(QCloseEvent *);
```

Then, let's define the closeEvent function in mainwindow.cpp, as follows:

```cpp
void MainWindow::closeEvent(QCloseEvent *e)
{
    QSettings sts;
    sts.setValue("MainGeometry", saveGeometry());
    sts.setValue("MainState", saveState());
    e->accept();
}
```

Remember to add `#include <QSettings>` in order to include the `QSettings` header files.

Thanks to `setOrganizationName` and `setApplicationName`, we don't need to pass any arguments to the `QSettings` constructor now. Instead, we call a `setValue` function to save the settings. The `saveGeometry()` and `saveState()` functions return the `MainWindow` geometry and state respectively as the `QByteArray` objects.

The next step is to read these settings and restore the geometry and state. This can be done inside the constructor of `MainWindow`. You just need to add two statements to it:

```
QSettings sts;
restoreGeometry(sts.value("MainGeometry").toByteArray());
restoreState(sts.value("MainState").toByteArray());
```

Here, `toByteArray()` can translate the stored value to a `QByteArray` object. How do we test to see if this works? To do this, perform the following steps:

1. Rebuild this application.
2. Run it.
3. Move its position.
4. Close it.
5. Run it again.

You'll see that the clock will appear at exactly the same position as it was before it closed. Now that you're pretty much familiar with widgets, layouts, settings, signals, and slots, it's time to cook a preference dialog by performing the following steps:

1. Right-click on the `Fancy_Clock` project in the **Projects** panel.
2. Select **Add New...**.
3. Select **Qt** in the **Files and Classes** panel.
4. Click on **Qt Designer Form Class** in the middle panel.
5. Select **Dialog with Buttons Bottom**.
6. Fill in `Preference` under **Class name**.
7. Click on **Next**, and then select **Finish**.

Qt Creator will redirect you to the **Design** mode. First, let's change `windowTitle` to **Preference**, and then do some UI work. Perform the following steps to do this:

1. Drag **Label** to `QDialog` and change its `objectName` property to `colourLabel`. Next, change its text to `Colour`.

2. Add **QComboBox** and change its `objectName` property to `colourBox`.

3. Add the `Black`, `White`, `Green`, and `Red` items to `colourBox`.

4. Change the layout of `Preference` to **Lay Out in a Form Lay Out**.

Close this UI file. Go back to editing the `preference.h` add a private `onAccepted` slot. The following code shows the content of this file:

```
#ifndef PREFERENCE_H
#define PREFERENCE_H

#include <QDialog>

namespace Ui {
  class Preference;
}

class Preference : public QDialog
{
  Q_OBJECT

public:
  explicit Preference(QWidget *parent = 0);
  ~Preference();

private:
  Ui::Preference *ui;

private slots:
  void onAccepted();
};

#endif // PREFERENCE_H
```

As usual, we define this slot in the source file. Besides, we have to set up some initializations in the constructor of `Preference`. Thus, `preference.cpp` becomes similar to the following code:

```cpp
#include <QSettings>
#include "preference.h"
#include "ui_preference.h"

Preference::Preference(QWidget *parent) :
  QDialog(parent),
  ui(new Ui::Preference)
{
  ui->setupUi(this);

  QSettings sts;
  ui->colourBox->setCurrentIndex(sts.value("Colour").toInt());

  connect(ui->buttonBox, &QDialogButtonBox::accepted, this,
    &Preference::onAccepted);
}

Preference::~Preference()
{
  delete ui;
}

void Preference::onAccepted()
{
  QSettings sts;
  sts.setValue("Colour", ui->colourBox->currentIndex());
}
```

Similarly, we load the settings and change the current item of `colourBox`. Then, it's the signal and slot coupling that follow. Note that Qt Creator has automatically generated the accept and reject connections between `buttonBox` and `Preference` for us. The `accepted` signal of `buttonBox` is emitted when the **OK** button is clicked. Likewise, the `rejected` signal is emitted if the user clicks on **Cancel**. You may want to check **Signals & Slots Editor** in the **Design** mode to see which connections are defined there. This is shown in the following screenshot:

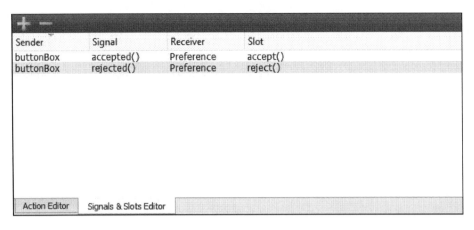

As for the definition of the `onAccepted` slot, it saves `currentIndex` of `colourBox` to the settings so that we can read this setting elsewhere.

Now, what we're going to do next is add an entry for `Preference` in the pop-up menu and change the color of `lcdNumber` according to the `Colour` setting value. Therefore, you should define a private slot and a private member function in `mainwindow.h` first.

```cpp
#ifndef MAINWINDOW_H
#define MAINWINDOW_H

#include <QMainWindow>

namespace Ui {
  class MainWindow;
}

class MainWindow : public QMainWindow
{
  Q_OBJECT
```

```
public:
  explicit MainWindow(QWidget *parent = 0);
  ~MainWindow();

private:
  Ui::MainWindow *ui;
  QPoint m_mousePos;
  void setColour();

private slots:
  void updateTime();
  void showContextMenu(const QPoint &pos);
  void showPreference();

protected:
  void mouseReleaseEvent(QMouseEvent *);
  void mousePressEvent(QMouseEvent *);
  void mouseMoveEvent(QMouseEvent *);
  void closeEvent(QCloseEvent *);
};


#endif // MAINWINDOW_H
```

The setColour function is used to change the color of lcdNumber, while the showPreference slot will execute a Preference object. The definitions of these two members are in the mainwindow.cpp file, which is displayed in the following manner:

```
#include <QTimer>
#include <QTime>
#include <QMouseEvent>
#include <QMenu>
#include <QAction>
#include <QSettings>
#include "mainwindow.h"
#include "preference.h"
#include "ui_mainwindow.h"

MainWindow::MainWindow(QWidget *parent) :
  QMainWindow(parent),
  ui(new Ui::MainWindow)
{
  ui->setupUi(this);
```

```cpp
  setAttribute(Qt::WA_TranslucentBackground);
  setWindowFlags(Qt::WindowStaysOnTopHint |
    Qt::FramelessWindowHint | windowFlags());

  QSettings sts;
  restoreGeometry(sts.value("MainGeometry").toByteArray());
  restoreState(sts.value("MainState").toByteArray());
  setColour();

  connect(this, &MainWindow::customContextMenuRequested, this,
    &MainWindow::showContextMenu);

  QTimer *timer = new QTimer(this);
  connect(timer, &QTimer::timeout, this, &MainWindow::updateTime);
  timer->start(1000);

  updateTime();
}

MainWindow::~MainWindow()
{
  delete ui;
}

void MainWindow::updateTime()
{
  QTime currentTime = QTime::currentTime();
  QString currentTimeText = currentTime.toString("hh:mm");
  if (currentTime.second() % 2 == 0) {
    currentTimeText[2] = ' ';
  }
  ui->lcdNumber->display(currentTimeText);
}

void MainWindow::showContextMenu(const QPoint &pos)
{
  QMenu contextMenu;
  contextMenu.addAction(QString("Preference"), this,
    SLOT(showPreference()));
  contextMenu.addAction(QString("Exit"), this, SLOT(close()));
  contextMenu.exec(mapToGlobal(pos));
}
```

```cpp
void MainWindow::mouseReleaseEvent(QMouseEvent *e)
{
  if (e->button() == Qt::RightButton) {
    emit customContextMenuRequested(e->pos());
  }
  else {
    QMainWindow::mouseReleaseEvent(e);
  }
}

void MainWindow::mousePressEvent(QMouseEvent *e)
{
  m_mousePos = e->pos();
}

void MainWindow::mouseMoveEvent(QMouseEvent *e)
{
  this->move(e->globalPos() - m_mousePos);
}

void MainWindow::closeEvent(QCloseEvent *e)
{
  QSettings sts;
  sts.setValue("MainGeometry", saveGeometry());
  sts.setValue("MainState", saveState());
  e->accept();
}

void MainWindow::setColour()
{
  QSettings sts;
  int i = sts.value("Colour").toInt();
  QPalette c;
  switch (i) {
  case 0://black
    c.setColor(QPalette::Foreground, Qt::black);
    break;
  case 1://white
    c.setColor(QPalette::Foreground, Qt::white);
    break;
  case 2://green
    c.setColor(QPalette::Foreground, Qt::green);
    break;
```

```
  case 3://red
    c.setColor(QPalette::Foreground, Qt::red);
    break;
  }
  ui->lcdNumber->setPalette(c);
  this->update();
}

void MainWindow::showPreference()
{
  Preference *pre = new Preference(this);
  pre->exec();
  setColour();
}
```

We call `setColour` in the constructor in order to set the color of `lcdNumber` correctly. Inside `setColour`, we first read the `Colour` value from the settings, and then use a `switch` statement to get the correct `QPalette` class before calling `setPalette` to change the color of `lcdNumber`. Since Qt doesn't provide a direct way to change the foreground color of the `QLCDNumber` objects, we need to use this tedious method to achieve this. At the end of this member function, we call `update()` to update the `MainWindow` user interface.

 Don't forget to add the `Preference` action to `contextMenu` inside `showContextMenu`. Otherwise, there will be no way to open the dialog.

In the relevant `showPreference` slot, we create a new `Preference` object, which is the child of `MainWindow`, and then call `exec()` to execute and show it. Lastly, we call `setColour()` to change the color of `lcdNumber`. As `Preference` is modal and `exec()` has its own event loop, it will block the application until `pre` is finished. After `pre` finishes executing, either by `accepted` or `rejected`, `setColour` will be called next. Of course, you can use the signal-slot way to implement it, but we have to apply some modifications to the previous code. Firstly, delete the `accepted-accept` signal-slot couple in `preference.ui` in the **Design** mode. Then, add `accept()` to the end of `onAccepted` in `preference.cpp`.

```
void Preference::onAccepted()
{
  QSettings sts;
  sts.setValue("Colour", ui->colourBox->currentIndex());
  this->accept();
}
```

Now, showPreference in mainwindow.cpp can be rewritten as follows:

```cpp
void MainWindow::showPreference()
{
  Preference *pre = new Preference(this);
  connect(pre, &Preference::accepted, this,
    &MainWindow::setColour);
  pre->exec();
}
```

> The connect statement shouldn't be placed after exec(), as it will cause the binding to fail.

No matter which way you prefer, the clock should have a **Preference** dialog now. Run it, select **Preference** from the pop-up menu, and change the color to whatever you please. You should expect a result similar to what is shown in the following screenshot:

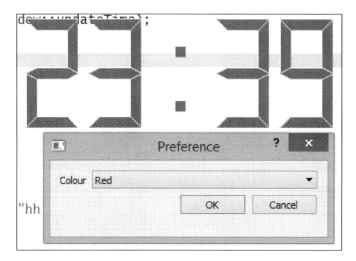

Building on the Unix platforms

So far, we are still trapped with our applications on Windows. It's time to test whether our code can be built on other platforms. In this chapter, the code involved with only desktop operating systems, while we'll get a chance to build applications for mobile platforms later in this book. In terms of other desktop operating systems, there are plenty of them, and most of them are Unix-like. Qt officially supports Linux and Mac OS X, along with Windows. Hence, users of other systems, such as **FreeBSD**, may need to compile Qt from scratch or get prebuilt packages from their own communities. In this book, the Linux distribution **Fedora 20** is used as a demonstration to introduce platform crossing. Please bear in mind that there are lots of desktop environments and theming tools on Linux, so don't be surprised if the user interface differs. Well, since you're curious, let me tell you that the desktop environment is **KDE 4** with QtCurve, unifying GTK+ / Qt 4 / Qt 5 in my case. Let's get started as soon as you're ready. You can perform the following steps to do this:

1. Copy the source code of Fancy Clock to a directory under Linux.
2. Delete the Fancy_Clock.pro.user file.
3. Open this project in Qt Creator.

Now, build and run this application. Everything is good except that there's a taskbar icon. Small issues such as this can't be avoided without testing. Well, to fix this, just modify a single line in the constructor of MainWindow. Changing the window flags will amend this:

```
setWindowFlags(Qt::WindowStaysOnTopHint | Qt::FramelessWindowHint
    | Qt::Tool);
```

If you run the file again, Fancy Clock won't show up in the taskbar any more. Please keep the MainWindow object, w, as a child of QWidget wid; otherwise, the application won't terminate after you click on **Close**.

Note that the **Preference** dialog uses native UI controls, rather than bringing the other platform's controls to this one. This is one of the most fascinating things that Qt has provided. All the Qt applications will look and behave like native applications across all platforms.

It's not a hustle but the truth is that once you code the Qt application, you can run it everywhere. You don't need to write different GUIs for different platforms. That dark age has long gone. However, you may want to write some functions for specific platforms, either because of particular needs or workarounds. Firstly, I'd like to introduce you to some Qt Add-On modules dedicated for several platforms.

Take Qt Windows Extras as an example. Some cool features that Windows provides, such as **Thumbnail Toolbar** and **Aero Peek**, are supported by Qt through this add-on module.

Well, adding this module to the project file directly, which in this case is Fancy_ Clock.pro file, will definitely upset other platforms. A better way to do this is to test whether it's on Windows; if so, add this module to the project. Otherwise, skip this step. The following code shows you the Fancy_Clock.pro file, which will add the winextras module if it's built on Windows:

```
QT          += core gui

win32: QT += winextras

greaterThan(QT_MAJOR_VERSION, 4): QT += widgets

TARGET = Fancy_Clock
TEMPLATE = app


SOURCES += main.cpp\
    mainwindow.cpp \
```

```
    preference.cpp

HEADERS   += mainwindow.h \
    preference.h

FORMS     += mainwindow.ui \
    preference.ui
```

As you can see, `win32` is a conditional statement, which is `true` only if the host machine is Windows. After a `qmake` rerun for this project, you'll be able to include and utilize those extra classes.

Similarly, if you want to do something on the Unix platforms, simply use the keyword `unix`, but `unix` will be `true` only on Linux/X11 or Mac OS X. To distinguish Mac OS X from Linux, here's an example:

```
win32 {
   message("Built on Windows")
}
else: unix: macx{
   message("Built on Mac OS X")
}
else {
   message("Built on Linux")
}
```

In fact, you can just use `unix: !macx` as the conditional statement to do some platform-specific work on Linux. It's a common practice to have many platform-specific statements in the project file(s), especially when your project needs to be linked with other libraries. You have to specify different paths for these libraries on different platforms, otherwise the compiler will complain about missing libraries or unknown symbols.

In addition to this, you may want to know how to write platform-specific code while keeping it from other platforms. Similar to C++, it's a predefined macro that is handled by various compilers. However, these compiler macro lists may differ from one compiler to another. So, it is better to use `Global Qt Declarations` instead. I'll use a the following short example to explain this further:

```
void MainWindow::showContextMenu(const QPoint &pos)
{
  QMenu contextMenu;
  #ifdef Q_OS_WIN
  contextMenu.addAction(QString("Options"), this,
    SLOT(showPreference()));
```

```
  #elif defined(Q_OS_LINUX)
  contextMenu.addAction(QString("Profile"), this,
    SLOT(showPreference()));
  #else
  contextMenu.addAction(QString("Preference"), this,
    SLOT(showPreference()));
  #endif
  contextMenu.addAction(QString("Exit"), this, SLOT(close()));
  contextMenu.exec(mapToGlobal(pos));
}
```

The preceding code shows you the new version of showContextMenu. The Preference menu entry will use different texts on different platforms, namely Windows, Linux, and Mac OS X. Change your showContextMenu function and run it again. You'll see **Options** on Windows, **Profile** on Linux, and **Preference** on Mac OS X. Below is a list concerning the platform-specific macros. You can get a full description, including other macros, functions, and types on the QtGlobal document.

Macro	Correspond Platform
Q_OS_ANDROID	Android
Q_OS_FREEBSD	FreeBSD
Q_OS_LINUX	Linux
Q_OS_IOS	iOS
Q_OS_MAC	Mac OS X and iOS (Darwin-based)
Q_OS_WIN	All Windows platforms, including Windows CE
Q_OS_WINPHONE	Windows Phone 8
Q_OS_WINRT	Windows Runtime on Windows 8. Windows RT and Windows Phone 8

Summary

In this chapter, information, including some tricks, about UI designing is included. Furthermore, there are basic yet useful cross-platform topics. Now, you're able to write an elegant Qt application in your favorite, and possibly already mastered, C++.

In the next chapter, we are going to learn how to write an application in Qt Quick. However, fear not; Qt Quick is even easier and, of course, quicker to develop.

3
Cooking an RSS Reader with Qt Quick

In this chapter, we will focus on developing applications with Qt Quick. For touchscreen-enabled devices, Qt Quick applications are much more responsive and easy to write. An RSS reader is used as a demonstration in this chapter. The following topics will enable you to build elegant Qt Quick applications:

- Understanding model and view
- Parsing RSS Feeds by `XmlListModel`
- Tweaking the categories
- Utilizing `ScrollView`
- Adding `BusyIndicator`
- Making a frameless window
- Debugging QML

Understanding model and view

As mentioned before, Qt Quick applications are different from traditional Qt Widgets applications. You are going to write QML instead of C++ code. So, let's create a new project, a Qt Quick application named `RSS_Reader`. This time, we will use Qt Quick 2.3 as the component set. Since we won't use the widgets provided by Qt Quick Controls, we'll write our own widgets.

Before getting our hands dirty, let's sketch out what this application looks like. According to the following diagram, there will be two sections. The left-hand panel provides some categories so that users can choose interesting categories. The right-hand panel is the main area, which displays news under the current category. This is a typical RSS news reader's user interface.

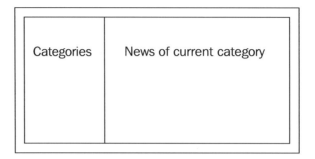

We can implement the **Categories** panel by using ListView. This type (we say "type" instead of "class" in QML) is used to display data from all sorts of list models. So let's edit our main.qml to something similar to this:

```
import QtQuick 2.3
import QtQuick.Window 2.2

Window {
    id: mainWindow
    visible: true
    width: 720
    height: 400

    ListView {
        id: categories

        width: 150
        height: parent.height
        orientation: ListView.Vertical
        anchors.top: parent.top
        spacing: 3
    }
}
```

`ListView` needs a model to get data from. In this case, we can utilize `ListModel` for its simplicity. To achieve this, let's create a new `Feeds.qml` file, which will contain a custom `ListModel` example:

1. Right-click on the project.
2. Select **Add New...**.
3. Navigate to **Qt | QML File (Qt Quick 2)**.
4. Enter the `Feeds.qml` filename.

Here is the content of `Feeds.qml`:

```
import QtQuick 2.3

ListModel {
  ListElement { name: "Top Stories"; url:
    "http://feeds.bbci.co.uk/news/rss.xml" }
  ListElement { name: "World"; url:
    "http://feeds.bbci.co.uk/news/world/rss.xml" }
  ListElement { name: "UK"; url:
    "http://feeds.bbci.co.uk/news/uk/rss.xml" }
  ListElement { name: "Business"; url:
    "http://feeds.bbci.co.uk/news/business/rss.xml" }
  ListElement { name: "Politics"; url:
    "http://feeds.bbci.co.uk/news/politics/rss.xml" }
  ListElement { name: "Health"; url:
    "http://feeds.bbci.co.uk/news/health/rss.xml" }
  ListElement { name: "Education & Family"; url:
    "http://feeds.bbci.co.uk/news/education/rss.xml" }
  ListElement { name: "Science & Environment"; url:
    "http://feeds.bbci.co.uk/news/science_and_environment/rss.xml"
      }
  ListElement { name: "Technology"; url:
    "http://feeds.bbci.co.uk/news/technology/rss.xml" }
  ListElement { name: "Entertainment & Arts"; url:
    "http://feeds.bbci.co.uk/news/entertainment_and_arts/rss.xml"
      }
}
```

 We use BBC News RSS as feeds, but you may wish to change it to another.

As you can see, the preceding `ListModel` example has two roles, `name` and `url`. A "role" is basically a fancy way of saying the child item. These can be bound to by the `ListView` delegate that we are about to create. In this way, roles usually represent the properties of an entity or columns of a table.

Let me explain the relation between view, model, and delegate, which is another important yet difficult concept in the world of Qt. This is officially called **model-view** architecture. In addition to the traditional view, Qt decouples the view and controller so that the data can be rendered and edited in many customized ways. The latter is much more elegant and efficient. The following diagram helps you understand this concept:

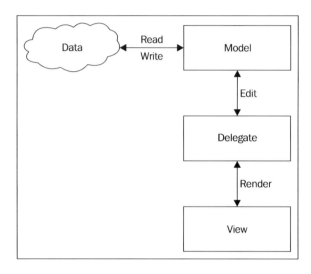

Take `ListModel`, which is a model used to arrange data, as an example to elaborate the relationship. `CategoriesDelegate`, shown in the following code, is a delegate and is used to control how to display the roles from the model. Lastly, we use a view, which is `ListView` in this case, to render the delegate.

The communication between the models, views, and delegates are based on the signals and slots mechanism. It'll take you some time to fully understand this concept. Hopefully, we can shorten this time by practicing this example. At this stage, we already have a view and a model. We have to define a delegate, which is `CategoriesDelegate` as mentioned before, to control the data from the model and render it on the view. Add a new `CategoriesDelegate.qml` file, whose content is pasted in this way:

```
import QtQuick 2.3

Rectangle {
```

```
  id: delegate
  property real itemWidth
  width: itemWidth
  height: 80
  Text {
    id: title
    anchors { left: parent.left; leftMargin: 10; right:
      parent.right; rightMargin: 10 }
    anchors.verticalCenter: delegate.verticalCenter
    text: name
    font { pointSize: 18; bold: true }
    verticalAlignment: Text.AlignVCenter
    wrapMode: Text.WordWrap
  }
}
```

You should have some idea about the relation between the model, delegate, and view. Here, we use Rectangle as the delegate type. Inside the Rectangle type is a Text object that displays the name from our ListModel example. As for the font property, here we use pointSize to specify the size of text, while you can use pixelSize as an alternative.

To finish the model-view architecture, go back to the main.qml edit:

```
import QtQuick 2.3
import QtQuick.Window 2.2
import "qrc:/"

Window {
  id: mainWindow
  visible: true
  width: 720
  height: 400

  Feeds {
    id: categoriesModel
  }

  ListView {
    id: categories

    width: 150
    height: parent.height
    orientation: ListView.Vertical
    anchors.top: parent.top
```

```
        spacing: 3
        model:categoriesModel
        delegate: CategoriesDelegate {
          id: categoriesDelegate
          width: categories.width
        }
      }
    }
  }
```

Take note of the third line; it's crucial to import this directory into `qrc`. We use `"qrc:/"` because we need to put the QML files in the root directory. Modify it if you use a subdirectory to keep `Feeds.qml` and `CategoriesDelegate.qml`. In this example, these files are left unorganized. But it's highly recommended to keep them categorized as a different module. If you didn't import the directory, you won't be able to use these QML files.

Inside the `Window` item, we create `Feeds`, which is exactly an element of `ListModel` from `Feeds.qml`. Then, we give this `Feeds` item a `categoriesModel` ID and use it as the model of `ListView`. Specifying the delegate is quite similar to specifying the model for views. Instead of declaring it outside `ListView`, we have to define it inside the `delegate` scope, otherwise the `delegate` item, `CategoriesDelegate`, won't be able to get data from the model. As you can see, we can manipulate the `width` of `categoriesDelegate`. This is to ensure that the text won't lie outside the boundary of `ListView`.

If everything is done correctly, click on **Run** and you'll see it run like this:

Parsing RSS Feeds by XmlListModel

It's true that we now have categories, but they don't seem to be involved with RSS at all. Also, if you dig deeper, you'll find that the RSS feeds are in fact the XML documents. Qt already provides a useful type to help us parse them. We don't need to reinvent the wheel. This powerful type is the so-called `XmlListModel` element and it uses `XmlRole` to query.

Firstly, we need to expose the `url` role of `categoriesModel` to the main scope. This is done by declaring the property storing the model's current element, `url`, inside `ListView`. Then, we can add an `XmlListModel` element and use that `url` element as its `source`. Accordingly, the modified `main.qml` file is pasted here:

```
import QtQuick 2.3
import QtQuick.Window 2.2
import QtQuick.XmlListModel 2.0
import "qrc:/"

Window {
   id: mainWindow
   visible: true
   width: 720
   height: 400

   Feeds {
      id: categoriesModel
   }

   ListView {
      id: categories
      width: 150
      height: parent.height
      orientation: ListView.Vertical
      anchors.top: parent.top
      spacing: 3
      model:categoriesModel
      delegate: CategoriesDelegate {
         id: categoriesDelegate
         width: categories.width
      }
      property string currentUrl: categoriesModel.get(0).url
   }
```

```
XmlListModel {
  id: newsModel

  source: categories.currentUrl
  namespaceDeclarations: "declare namespace media =
    'http://search.yahoo.com/mrss/'; declare namespace atom =
      'http://www.w3.org/2005/Atom';"
  query: "/rss/channel/item"

  XmlRole { name: "title"; query: "title/string()" }
  XmlRole { name: "description"; query: "description/string()" }
  XmlRole { name: "link"; query: "link/string()" }
  XmlRole { name: "pubDate"; query: "pubDate/string()" }
  //XPath starts from 1 not 0 and the second thumbnail is larger
    and more clear
  XmlRole { name: "thumbnail"; query:
    "media:thumbnail[2]/@url/string()" }
  }
}
```

 Objects' values are changed dynamically and updated implicitly in
Qt Quick. You don't need to give new values explicitly.

In order to use this element, you will need to import the module by adding an
`import QtQuick.XmlListModel 2.0` line. Additionally, `XmlListModel` is a read-
only model which means that you can't modify the data source through this model.
This is completely acceptable since what we need is to retrieve the news data from
the RSS feeds. Take `Top Stories` as an example; the following code is a part of this
XML document content:

```
<?xml version="1.0" encoding="UTF-8"?>
<?xml-stylesheet title="XSL_formatting" type="text/xsl"
  href="/shared/bsp/xsl/rss/nolsol.xsl"?>

<rss xmlns:media="http://search.yahoo.com/mrss/"
  xmlns:atom="http://www.w3.org/2005/Atom" version="2.0">
<channel>
<title>BBC News - Home</title>
<link>http://www.bbc.co.uk/news/#sa-ns_mchannel=rss&amp;
  ns_source=PublicRSS20-sa</link>
<description>The latest stories from the Home section of the BBC
  News web site.</description>
<language>en-gb</language>
<lastBuildDate>Mon, 26 Jan 2015 23:19:42 GMT</lastBuildDate>
```

```
<copyright>Copyright: (C) British Broadcasting Corporation, see
    http://news.bbc.co.uk/2/hi/help/rss/4498287.stm for terms and
        conditions of reuse.</copyright>
<image>
    <url>http://news.bbcimg.co.uk/nol/shared/img/bbc_news_120x60.gif
        </url>
    <title>BBC News - Home</title>
    <link>http://www.bbc.co.uk/news/#sa-ns_mchannel=rss&amp;
        ns_source=PublicRSS20-sa</link>
    <width>120</width>
    <height>60</height>
</image>
<ttl>15</ttl>
<atom:link href="http://feeds.bbci.co.uk/news/rss.xml" rel="self"
    type="application/rss+xml"/>
<item>
    <title>Germany warns Greece over debts</title>
    <description>The German government warns Greece that it must
        meet its commitments to lenders, after the election win of the
            Greek anti-austerity Syriza party.</description>
    <link>http://www.bbc.co.uk/news/
        business-30977714#sa-ns_mchannel=rss&amp;
            ns_source=PublicRSS20-sa</link>
    <guid isPermaLink="false">http://www.bbc.co.uk/news/
        business-30977714</guid>
    <pubDate>Mon, 26 Jan 2015 20:15:56 GMT</pubDate>
    <media:thumbnail width="66" height="49"
        url="http://news.bbcimg.co.uk/media/images/80536000/jpg/
            _80536447_025585607-1.jpg"/>
    <media:thumbnail width="144" height="81"
        url="http://news.bbcimg.co.uk/media/images/80536000/jpg/
            _80536448_025585607-1.jpg"/>
</item>
......
```

The `namespaceDeclarations` property needs to be set because the XML document has the XML namespaces.

```
<rss xmlns:media="http://search.yahoo.com/mrss/"
    xmlns:atom="http://www.w3.org/2005/Atom" version="2.0">
```

Here, `xmlns` stands for the XML namespace, so we declare the namespace accordingly.

```
namespaceDeclarations: "declare namespace media = 'http://search.
yahoo.com/mrss/'; declare namespace atom = 'http://www.w3.org/2005/
Atom';"
```

In fact, you can just declare a `media` namespace and safely ignore an `atom` namespace. However, if you didn't declare the `media` namespace, the application would end up failing to parse the XML document. Hence, go back to see the XML document and you'll find it has a hierarchy to order data. What we want here are these items. Take the top-level as root, `/`, so the path of `item` can be written as `/rss/channel/item`. This is exactly what we put in `query`.

All the `XmlRole` elements are created using `query` as the base. For `XmlRole`, `name` defines its name, which doesn't need to be the same as in the XML document. It's similar to `id` for the regular Qt Quick items. However, the query of `XmlRole` must use a relative path to the query of `XmlListModel`. Although it's a `string()` type in most cases, it still must be declared explicitly. If there are elements sharing the same keys, it'd be an array where the element listed first has the first index.

 The first index in XPath is 1 instead of 0.

Sometimes, we need to get an attribute `thumbnail`. This is the `url` attribute of the `media:thumbnail` tag. In this case, it's the `@` symbol that will do all the magic we need.

Similar to these categories, we have to write a delegate for the `XmlListModel` element to render the view. The new QML `NewsDelegate.qml` file is shown here:

```
import QtQuick 2.3

Column {
    id: news
    spacing: 8

    //used to separate news item
    Item { height: news.spacing; width: news.width }

    Row {
        width: parent.width
        height: children.height
        spacing: news.spacing

        Image {
            id: titleImage
            source: thumbnail
        }
```

```
      Text {
        width: parent.width - titleImage.width
        wrapMode: Text.WordWrap
        font.pointSize: 20
        font.bold: true
        text: title
      }
    }

    Text {
      width: parent.width
      font.pointSize: 9
      font.italic: true
      text: pubDate + " (<a href=\"" + link + "\">Details</a>)"
      onLinkActivated: {
        Qt.openUrlExternally(link)
      }
    }

    Text {
      width: parent.width
      wrapMode: Text.WordWrap
      font.pointSize: 10.5
      horizontalAlignment: Qt.AlignLeft
      text: description
    }
  }
}
```

The difference is that this time we use `Column` to organize the news data and represent it in an intuitive way. The relevant diagram is sketched as follows:

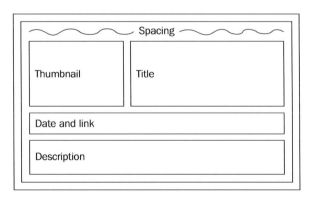

So, this is why we use `Row` inside `Column` to box **Thumbnail** and **Title** together. Thus, we need to put an empty `item` element in front to separate each news delegate. Apart from these self-explanatory lines, there is a tip for dealing with links. You need to specify the slot for the `onLinkActivated` signal, which is `Qt.openUrlExternally(link)` in this case. Otherwise, nothing will happen when you click on the link.

After all this, it's time to write a view in `main.qml` to display our news:

```qml
import QtQuick 2.3
import QtQuick.Window 2.2
import QtQuick.XmlListModel 2.0
import "qrc:/"

Window {
  id: mainWindow
  visible: true
  width: 720
  height: 400

  Feeds {
    id: categoriesModel
  }

  ListView {
    id: categories

    width: 150
    height: parent.height
    orientation: ListView.Vertical
    anchors.top: parent.top
    spacing: 3
    model:categoriesModel
    delegate: CategoriesDelegate {
      id: categoriesDelegate
      width: categories.width
    }
    property string currentUrl: categoriesModel.get(0).url
  }

  XmlListModel {
    id: newsModel
```

```
    source: categories.currentUrl
    namespaceDeclarations: "declare namespace media =
      'http://search.yahoo.com/mrss/'; declare namespace atom =
        'http://www.w3.org/2005/Atom';"
    query: "/rss/channel/item"

    XmlRole { name: "title"; query: "title/string()" }
    XmlRole { name: "description"; query: "description/string()" }
    XmlRole { name: "link"; query: "link/string()" }
    XmlRole { name: "pubDate"; query: "pubDate/string()" }
    //XPath starts from 1 not 0 and the second thumbnail is larger
      and more clear
    XmlRole { name: "thumbnail"; query:
      "media:thumbnail[2]/@url/string()" }
  }

  ListView {
    id: newsList

    anchors { left: categories.right; leftMargin: 10; right:
      parent.right; rightMargin: 4; top: parent.top; bottom:
        parent.bottom; }
    model: newsModel
    delegate: NewsDelegate {
      width: newsList.width
    }
  }
}
```

Remember to define the `width` of `NewsDelegate` in case it displays abnormally. Click on **Run**; the application will look like the following screenshot:

Tweaking the categories

This application is still incomplete. For example, the news view won't change at all after you click on the other categories. In this stage, we're going to work this out and make it more beautiful.

What we need to do is add `MouseArea` to `CategoriesDelegate`. This element is used to deal with a variety of mouse interactions, including clicking. The new `CategoriesDelegate.qml` file's code is pasted here:

```
import QtQuick 2.3

Rectangle {
  id: delegate
  height: 80

  Text {
    id: title
    anchors { left: parent.left; leftMargin: 10; right:
      parent.right; rightMargin: 10 }
    anchors.verticalCenter: delegate.verticalCenter
    text: name
    font { pointSize: 18; bold: true }
    verticalAlignment: Text.AlignVCenter
    wrapMode: Text.WordWrap
  }

  MouseArea {
    anchors.fill: delegate
    onClicked: {
      categories.currentIndex = index
      if(categories.currentUrl == url)
      newsModel.reload()
      else
      categories.currentUrl = url
    }
  }
}
```

As you can see, once a delegate gets clicked on, it'll change `categories.currentIndex` and `currentUrl` if necessary, or simply let `newsModel` reload. As mentioned before, QML is a dynamic language, which changes `categories.currentUrl`, the `source` property of `newsModel`, and would automatically cause `newsModel` to reload.

To help users distinguish a currently-selected category from others, we may wish to change its size and scale. There are some attached properties, which are attached to each instance of a delegate or are simply shared among them. The `.isCurrentItem` property is the one that would so us a favor. It's a Boolean value that holds whether this delegate is the current item or not. However, only the root item of a delegate can access these attached properties directly. In order to code in a clean way, we add a line to `Rectangle` of `CategoriesDelegate` to hold this property:

```
property bool selected: ListView.isCurrentItem
```

Now, we can utilize `selected` in `Text` by adding the following lines to the `Text` item:

```
scale: selected ? 1.0 : 0.8
color: selected ? "#000" : "#AAA"
```

`Text` will be scaled to `0.8` if it's not selected and will behave as usual when it's active. A similar condition is in place for its color. The `#AAA` color code is an extremely light gray color, which makes the active black text stand out more. However, there is no animation for these changes. While we want these transitions to be more natural, Qt Quick provides **Behavior with State** to make these transitions happen. By adding these lines to the `Text` item, we get the following code:

```
Behavior on color { ColorAnimation { duration: 300 } }
Behavior on scale { PropertyAnimation { duration: 300 } }
```

Animations are expected to present when you change the current delegate, which results in changes in the color and scale. If you're not sure whether you've performed the correct modification, the following code shows you the newly modified `CategoriesDelegate.qml` file:

```
import QtQuick 2.3

Rectangle {
    id: delegate
    height: 80

    property bool selected: ListView.isCurrentItem

    Text {
        id: title
        anchors { left: parent.left; leftMargin: 10; right:
            parent.right; rightMargin: 10 }
        anchors.verticalCenter: delegate.verticalCenter
        text: name
        font { pointSize: 18; bold: true }
```

```
        verticalAlignment: Text.AlignVCenter
        wrapMode: Text.WordWrap
        scale: selected ? 1.0 : 0.8
        color: selected ? "#000" : "#AAA"
        Behavior on color { ColorAnimation { duration: 300 } }
        Behavior on scale { PropertyAnimation { duration: 300 } }
    }

    MouseArea {
      anchors.fill: delegate
      onClicked: {
        categories.currentIndex = index
        if(categories.currentUrl == url)
        newsModel.reload()
        else
        categories.currentUrl = url
      }
    }
  }
}
```

There is room to improve the categories, including the background image which is simply an Image element, and could form part of your exercises. However, it won't be covered in this chapter. Here, what we do next is to change the displaying fonts on the Windows platform. We're going to change the font to Times New Roman by adding a few lines in main.cpp (not main.qml).

```
#include <QGuiApplication>
#include <QQmlApplicationEngine>
#include <QFont>

int main(int argc, char *argv[])
{
  QGuiApplication app(argc, argv);

  #ifdef Q_OS_WIN
  app.setFont(QFont(QString("Times New Roman")));
  #endif

  QQmlApplicationEngine engine;
  engine.load(QUrl(QStringLiteral("qrc:/main.qml")));

  return app.exec();
}
```

Here, we use a predefined macro to limit this change for the Windows platforms. By setting the font of app whose type is QGuiApplication, all the children widgets, including engine, are subjected to this change. Now run the application again; you should expect a new RSS reader with this newspaper-like font:

Utilizing ScrollView

Our RSS news reader is shaping up now. From now on, let's focus on the unpleasant details. The first thing we're going to add is a scroll bar. To be more specific, ScrollView is about to be added.

Back in the Qt 4 era, you had to write your own ScrollView component to gain this small yet very nice feature. Although you can utilize KDE Plasma Components' ScrollArea on X11 Platforms, there are no Qt bundled modules for this purpose, which means you can't use these on Windows and Mac OS X. Thanks to the open governance of the Qt project, a lot of community code gets merged, especially from the KDE community. From Qt 5.1 onwards, we have the QtQuick.Controls module, which has many built-in desktop components, including ScrollView.

It's a very easy to use element that provides scroll bars and content frames for its child item. There can be only one direct Item child, and this child is implicitly anchored to fill the ScrollView component. This means that we only need to anchor the ScrollView component.

There are two ways to specify the child item. The first one is to declare the child item inside the ScrollView component's scope, and the item which is inside will implicitly become the child of the ScrollView component. Another way is to set the contentItem property, which is an explicit method. In this chapter's example, both ways are demonstrated for you. The content of main.qml is shown here:

```
import QtQuick 2.3
import QtQuick.Window 2.2
import QtQuick.XmlListModel 2.0
import QtQuick.Controls 1.2
import QtQuick.Controls.Styles 1.2
import "qrc:/"

Window {
  id: mainWindow
  visible: true
  width: 720
  height: 400

  Feeds {
    id: categoriesModel
  }

  ListView {
    id: categories

    orientation: ListView.Vertical
    spacing: 3
    model:categoriesModel
    delegate: CategoriesDelegate {
      id: categoriesDelegate
      width: categories.width
    }
    property string currentUrl: categoriesModel.get(0).url
  }

  ScrollView {
    id: categoriesView
    contentItem: categories
    anchors { left: parent.left; top: parent.top; bottom:
      parent.bottom; }
    width: 0.2 * parent.width
```

```
    style: ScrollViewStyle {
      transientScrollBars: true
    }
  }
}


XmlListModel {
id: newsModel

source: categories.currentUrl
namespaceDeclarations: "declare namespace media =
   'http://search.yahoo.com/mrss/'; declare namespace atom =
      'http://www.w3.org/2005/Atom';"
query: "/rss/channel/item"

XmlRole { name: "title"; query: "title/string()" }
XmlRole { name: "description"; query: "description/string()" }
XmlRole { name: "link"; query: "link/string()" }
XmlRole { name: "pubDate"; query: "pubDate/string()" }
//XPath starts from 1 not 0 and the second thumbnail is larger
   and more clear
XmlRole { name: "thumbnail"; query:
   "media:thumbnail[2]/@url/string()" }
}

ScrollView {
  id: newsView
  anchors { left: categoriesView.right; leftMargin: 10; right:
    parent.right; top: parent.top; bottom: parent.bottom }
  style: ScrollViewStyle {
    transientScrollBars: true
  }
  ListView {
    id: newsList
    model: newsModel
    delegate: NewsDelegate {
      width: newsList.width
    }
  }
 }
}
```

Since the child item is automatically filled with `anchors`, some lines inside `ListView` are deleted. Most of them are just moved to `ScrollView` though. You can see that we use the explicit way for `categories` and the implicit way for `newsList`.

Looking into `ScrollView`, we defined a custom `style` element by forcing `transientScrollBars` to `true`. It's noted that the default value of `transientScrollBars` is platform dependent. The transient scroll bars only appear when the content is scrolled and then disappear when they are no longer needed. Anyway, it's `false` by default on Windows, so we turn it on explicitly, resulting in a better visual style shown as follows:

Adding BusyIndicator

The absence of a busy indicator makes people uncomfortable as well. No matter how short or long indicator it is, it takes time to download data and parse XML. I'm pretty sure you'd like to add such an indicator, which tells users to calm down and wait. Luckily, `BusyIndicator`, which is simply a running circle, is an element of `QtQuick.Controls`. This does exactly what we want.

What you need to do is to add these lines to `main.qml` inside the `Window` item:

```
BusyIndicator {
    anchors.centerIn: newsView
    running: newsModel.status == XmlListModel.Loading
}
```

Note that we don't need to change the `visible` property of `BusyIndicator`, because `BusyIndicator` is only visible when the `running` property is set to `true`. In this case, we set `running` to `true` when the `newsModel` status is `Loading`.

Making a frameless window

Similar to what we did in the previous chapter, here we don't want the borders of the system window to decorate our Qt Quick application. This is partly because it looks like a web application, which makes it seems odd with native window decorations. This job is even easier in QML than in C++. We can add the following line to `Window` in `main.qml`:

```
flags: Qt.Window | Qt.FramelessWindowHint
```

Although our RSS reader runs in a frameless style, there is no way to move it and it's difficult to close it, just like the situation in the previous chapter. Since our mouse has many duties for the categories and news `ListView` along with `ScrollView`, we can't simply use a new `MouseArea` element to fill the `Window` root. Therefore, what we're going to do is to draw our own title bar and, of course, the exit button.

To add the exit button image to the `qrc` file, right-click on `qml.qrc`, select **Open in Editor**, navigate to **Add | Add Files**, and then select `close.png`.

 It'd be better to use different resource files (`qrc`) for different types of files, which make it more organized. We'll talk more about resource files in *Chapter 8, Enabling Your Qt Application to Support Other Languages*.

Now, add a new QML `TitleBar.qml` file whose content is pasted here:

```qml
import QtQuick 2.3

Row {
    id: titlebar
    width: parent.width
    height: 22
    layoutDirection: Qt.RightToLeft

    property point mPos: Qt.point(0,0)

    Image {
        id: closebutton
        width: 22
        height: 22
        fillMode: Image.PreserveAspectFit
```

```
      source: "qrc:/close.png"

    MouseArea {
      anchors.fill: parent
      onClicked: {
        Qt.quit()
      }
    }
  }

  Rectangle {
    width: titlebar.width - closebutton.width
    height: titlebar.height
    color: "#000"

    MouseArea {
      anchors.fill: parent
      onPressed: {
        mPos = Qt.point(mouseX, mouseY)
      }
      onPositionChanged: {
        mainWindow.setX(mainWindow.x + mouseX - mPos.x)
        mainWindow.setY(mainWindow.y + mouseY - mPos.y)
      }
    }
  }
}
```

Here, we use a QPoint object, mPos, to store the position when the mouse button is clicked.

> Although we may have declared it as var or variant in the past, for maximum performance you should avoid the use of var. Also note that variant is deprecated now, so it shouldn't be used under any circumstances.

The MouseArea element, which is used for moving, is located inside the Rectangle element. There are lots of predefined signals and slots for MouseArea. Note that we use the onPressed slot instead of onClicked here to get the mouse position. This is because the clicked signal is only emitted when the mouse button is pressed and then released, which makes it unsuitable for moving the window.

The `positionChanged` signal is emitted when the mouse button is pressed and then moved. In addition to this, there is a property called `hoverEnabled`, which is `false` by default. If you set it to `true`, all the mouse events will be handled even when no mouse button is clicked. In other words, the `positionChanged` signal will be emitted when the mouse is moving, regardless of whether it's clicked or not. Therefore, we don't set `hoverEnabled` to `true` in this example.

Now let's go back and check the `Image` item. The `fillMode` element determines how an image should be adjusted. By default, it'll be stretched despite the ratio. Here, we set it to preserve the ratio while we fit the `Image`. The `source` property holds the image file path. In this case, it's the `close.png` file that is in the `Resources` file, `qml.qrc`. Here we go; this is another `MouseArea`, which simply makes `Image` into a closed button.

At last, it's time to add `TitleBar` to `main.qml` as follows:

```
import QtQuick 2.3
import QtQuick.Window 2.2
import QtQuick.XmlListModel 2.0
import QtQuick.Controls 1.2
import QtQuick.Controls.Styles 1.2
import "qrc:/"

Window {
    id: mainWindow
    visible: true
    width: 720
    height: 400
    flags: Qt.Window | Qt.FramelessWindowHint

    TitleBar {
        id: titleBar
    }

    Text {
        id: windowTitle
        anchors { left: titleBar.left; leftMargin: 10; verticalCenter:
            titleBar.verticalCenter }
        text: "BBC News Reader"
        color: "#FFF"
        font.pointSize: 10
    }
```

```
Feeds {
  id: categoriesModel
}

ListView {
  id: categories

  orientation: ListView.Vertical
  spacing: 3
  model:categoriesModel
  delegate: CategoriesDelegate {
    id: categoriesDelegate
    width: categories.width
  }
  property string currentUrl: categoriesModel.get(0).url
}

ScrollView {
  id: categoriesView
  contentItem: categories
  anchors { left: parent.left; top: titleBar.bottom; bottom:
    parent.bottom; }
  width: 0.2 * parent.width
  style: ScrollViewStyle {
    transientScrollBars: true
  }
}

XmlListModel {
  id: newsModel

  source: categories.currentUrl
  namespaceDeclarations: "declare namespace media =
    'http://search.yahoo.com/mrss/'; declare namespace atom =
      'http://www.w3.org/2005/Atom';"
  query: "/rss/channel/item"

  XmlRole { name: "title"; query: "title/string()" }
  XmlRole { name: "description"; query: "description/string()" }
```

```
    XmlRole { name: "link"; query: "link/string()" }
    XmlRole { name: "pubDate"; query: "pubDate/string()" }
    //XPath starts from 1 not 0 and the second thumbnail is larger
      and more clear
    XmlRole { name: "thumbnail"; query:
      "media:thumbnail[2]/@url/string()" }
  }

  ScrollView {
    id: newsView
    anchors { left: categoriesView.right; leftMargin: 10; right:
      parent.right; top: titleBar.bottom; bottom: parent.bottom }
    style: ScrollViewStyle {
      transientScrollBars: true
    }
    ListView {
      id: newsList
      model: newsModel
      delegate: NewsDelegate {
        width: newsList.width
      }
    }
  }

  BusyIndicator {
    anchors.centerIn: newsView
    running: newsModel.status == XmlListModel.Loading
  }
}
```

We also use a Text element, windowTitle, to display the window title in titleBar.
Since we retrieve data from BBC News, it's not a bad idea to call it BBC News Reader
or just name it whatever you like.

Apart from the addition of the title bar, some code needs to be modified to spare
room for it. Both the ScrollView component's anchored top should be changed
to titleBar.bottom instead of parent.top, otherwise the title bar will be placed
partially on top of these two scroll views.

Give the application a run; it should deliver a new visual style. Although it looks more like a web application, the whole interface is clean and integrated. Another benefit of this change is a unified UI across all platforms.

Debugging QML

The most common practice to debug QML is the use of the API console. JavaScript developers should be familiar with this because of the console support in QML. The relationships between the `console` functions and the Qt/C++ `QDebug` functions are given as follows:

QML	Qt/C++
`console.log()`	`qDebug()`
`console.debug()`	`qDebug()`
`console.info()`	`qDebug()`
`console.warn()`	`qWarning()`
`console.error()`	`qCritical()`

With the preceding supports present, QML is just like JavaScript programming. At the same time, the following functions are also introduced in QML:

Functions	Description
console.assert()	This function tests whether the expression is true. If not, it will write an optional message to the console and print the stack trace.
console.exception()	This function prints an error message together with the stack trace of the JavaScript execution at the point it is called.
console.trace()	This function prints the stack trace of the JavaScript execution at the point it is called.
console.count()	This function prints the current number of times a particular piece of code has been executed, along with a message.
console.time() console.timeEnd()	This pair of functions will print the time that a particular piece of code between them takes in milliseconds.
console.profile() console.profileEnd()	This pair of functions profiles both the state of QDeclarativeEngine as well as the V8 call methods. However, you need to attach the QML Profiler tool to the application before console.profileEnd() is called.

In addition to the preceding useful functions, the common **Debug** mode in Qt Creator is available for QML as well. The operations are almost identical to C++ debugging. You can set the breakpoints, observe values, and so on. However, there is one more thing provided for QML. It's the **QML/JS Console**! Qt Creator doesn't show the **QML/JS Console** by default, you have to turn it on manually. Just click on the small button (the red circle in the following screenshot), and then tick **QML/JS Console**:

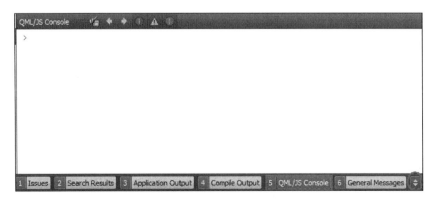

When the application is interrupted by a breakpoint, you can use the **QML/JS Console** to execute the JavaScript expressions in the current context. You can change the property values temporarily, without editing the source, and view the results in the running application.

The **QML/JS Console** tab shows the debug output, both the Qt debug messages and JavaScript console messages, in an appealing way. It provides a button group to help you filter information, warnings, and errors. Therefore, just use this **QML/JS Console** tab to replace **Application Output** when you debug Qt Quick applications.

Summary

In this chapter, we went through a thorough introduction to Qt Quick. We also covered model-view programming, which is a vital concept in both Qt/C++ and Qt Quick/QML. You may also find that QML is in some way an extensible version of JavaScript. This is an additional bonus for JavaScript developers. However, it's not difficult to start if you've never written a script before. Once you start, you'll get to explore the fascinating qualities of Qt Quick. We're going to show you how to access camera devices using Qt in the next chapter.

4
Controlling Camera and Taking Photos

Through this chapter, you'll find how easy it is to access and control a camera with Qt. The example in this chapter also demonstrates how to utilize the status bar and menu bar. In addition to the traditional Qt Widget applications, there is a QML camera example, which does the same thing as Qt/C++ but in a more elegant way. The following topics, which are covered in this chapter, will extend your application:

- Accessing the camera in Qt
- Controlling the camera
- Displaying errors in the status bar
- Displaying the permanent widgets in the status bar
- Utilizing the menu bar
- Using QFileDialog
- Using the QML Camera

Accessing the camera in Qt

Although we won't talk about the technical details of how a camera works, the overview of the implementation of a camera in Qt will be covered. Support for a camera is included in Qt Multimedia, which is a module that provides a rich set of QML types and C++ classes to handle multimedia content. Things such as audio playback, camera, and radio functionality are shown. To complement this, the Qt Multimedia Widgets module provides widget-based multimedia classes to make the work easier.

There are some classes to help us deal with the camera. For instance, `viewfinder` lets a user look through the camera to compose, and in many cases focus, the picture. In Qt/C++, you can use `QGraphicsView` along with `QGraphicsVideoItem` to do this job. `QGraphicsView` provides a widget to display the contents of `QGraphicsScene`. In this case, `QGraphicsVideoItem` is an item of the scene. This view-scene-item is the **Graphics View Framework**. For details on this concept, visit `http://doc.qt.io/ qt-5/graphicsview.html`. In this example, we use `QCameraViewfinder`, which is the dedicated `viewfinder` class and is simpler and more straightforward.

To capture a photo, we need to use the `QCameraImageCapture` class, which records the media content, while the focus and zoom are managed by the `QCameraFocus` class.

After all, `QCamera` plays a core role in this process. The `QCamera` class provides an interface to access the camera devices, including webcams and mobile device cameras. There is another class, `QCameraInfo`, which can list all the available camera devices and choose which one to use. The following diagram will help you understand this:

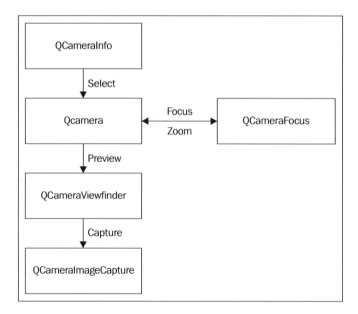

To see a demonstration, create a new Qt Widget Application project named CameraDemo. Edit the CameraDemo.pro file. Add multimedia multimediawidgets to QT by appending a line, as shown here, or add two modules to the predefined QT line:

```
QT        += multimedia multimediawidgets
```

After this modification, you need save the file and navigate to **Build | Run qmake** to load these new modules. Let's edit the mainwindow.ui file of CameraDemo to add some widgets to use the camera by performing the following steps:

1. Remove the status and menu bars. They will be re-added in the next sections. For now, they're removed for a cleaner user interface.

2. Drag **Widget** into the frame.

3. Change its name to viewfinder.

4. Right-click on viewfinder and select **Promote to ....**

5. Fill in QCameraViewfinder in the **Promoted class name** field. Remember to tick the **Global include** checkbox because this is a predefined Qt class. Click on **Add**, and then on **Promote**.

6. Set **MainWindow** to **Lay Out Horizontally**.

7. Drag a **Vertical** layout on the right-hand side of viewfinder. Following this, components will be added to the layout.

8. Add **Label**, which is used to display the captured image. Note that, here we don't use QGraphicsView, simply because QLabel is good enough for this purpose and is much easier.

9. Rename it as previewLabel and clear its text.

10. Drag **Combo Box** just beneath previewLabel.

11. Rename it as cameraComboBox since it'll be used to display all the available camera devices.

12. Add a **Push Button** named captureButton below ComboBox in the **Vertical** layout to let the user click to take a photo. This button should have the text Capture on it.

It should look like the following screenshot:

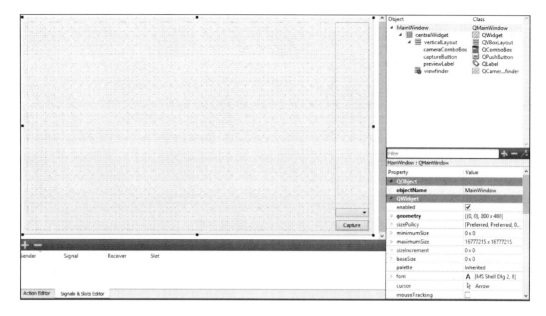

Now, go back to the `mainwindow.h` edit, as shown here:

```
#ifndef MAINWINDOW_H
#define MAINWINDOW_H

#include <QMainWindow>
#include <QCamera>
#include <QCameraInfo>
#include <QCameraImageCapture>

namespace Ui {
    class MainWindow;
}

class MainWindow : public QMainWindow
{
    Q_OBJECT

public:
    explicit MainWindow(QWidget *parent = 0);
    ~MainWindow();
```

```
private:
  Ui::MainWindow *ui;
  QList<QCameraInfo> camList;
  QCamera *camera;
  QCameraImageCapture *imgCapture;

private slots:
  void onCameraChanged(int);
  void onCaptureButtonClicked();
  void onImageCaptured(int, const QImage &);
};
```

```
#endif // MAINWINDOW_H
```

As usual, in order to use the classes in the preceding code, we have to include them properly. In addition to this, we use camList, which is a type of QList<QCameraInfo>, to store the available camera devices. Since QList is a template class, we have to pass the type of list element, which is QCameraInfo in this case, to the constructor.

These private slots are responsible for the camera controls, namely, changing the camera device and clicking the capture button. Meanwhile, onImageCaptured is used to handle the imageCaptured signal of QCameraImageCapture.

The content of the maindow.cpp file is shown as follows:

```
#include "mainwindow.h"
#include "ui_mainwindow.h"

MainWindow::MainWindow(QWidget *parent) :
  QMainWindow(parent),
  ui(new Ui::MainWindow)
{
  ui->setupUi(this);

  camera = NULL;
  connect(ui->captureButton, &QPushButton::clicked, this,
    &MainWindow::onCaptureButtonClicked);
  connect(ui->cameraComboBox, static_cast<void (QComboBox::*)
    (int)>(&QComboBox::currentIndexChanged), this,
      &MainWindow::onCameraChanged);

  camList = QCameraInfo::availableCameras();
  for (QList<QCameraInfo>::iterator it = camList.begin(); it !=
    camList.end(); ++it) {
```

```
      ui->cameraComboBox->addItem(it->description());
    }
}

MainWindow::~MainWindow()
{
   delete ui;
}

void MainWindow::onCameraChanged(int idx)
{
   if (camera != NULL) {
      camera->stop();
   }

   camera = new QCamera(camList.at(idx), this);
   camera->setViewfinder(ui->viewfinder);
   camera->setCaptureMode(QCamera::CaptureStillImage);
   camera->start();
}

void MainWindow::onCaptureButtonClicked()
{
   imgCapture = new QCameraImageCapture(camera, this);
   connect(imgCapture, &QCameraImageCapture::imageCaptured, this,
      &MainWindow::onImageCaptured);
   camera->searchAndLock();
   imgCapture->setCaptureDestination
      (QCameraImageCapture::CaptureToFile);
   imgCapture->capture();
}

void MainWindow::onImageCaptured(int, const QImage &img)
{
   QPixmap pix = QPixmap::fromImage(img).scaled(ui->previewLabel-
      >size(), Qt::KeepAspectRatio);
   ui->previewLabel->setPixmap(pix);
   camera->unlock();
   imgCapture->deleteLater();
}
```

Let's have a look at the constructor first. We give camera a NULL address to mark that there is no camera allocated and/or active. This is explained later.

Since there are overloaded signal functions for `QComboBox::currentIndexChanged`, you have to specify the signal that you want with `static_cast`. Otherwise, the compiler would complain and fail to compile. Only the new syntax statement of the signal and slot are affected, which means the old syntax statement, shown here, won't pose any errors:

```
connect(ui->cameraComboBox, SIGNAL(currentIndexChanged(int)),
    this, SLOT(onCameraChanged(int)));
```

However, as mentioned previously, the new syntax has many advantages and it's highly recommended that you replace the old one.

As we continue, we can fill in `camList` with the available cameras since `availableCameras` is a static member function of `QCameraInfo`, which returns a list of all available cameras on the system. Also, you can pass an argument to specify the camera position, such as the front or back camera, which is pretty useful on mobile platforms.

Then, we add all the items in `camList` to our camera `combobox`. Here, it's the iterator that walks through the list and operates each one. Using iterators is very fast when dealing with a list, array, and so on. Qt supports this method, including both Java-style and STL-style iterators. In this case, we prefer and use STL-style iterators. The description function of `QCameraInfo` returns a human-readable description of the camera.

Now, let's go inside `onCameraChanged`. Before the construction of the camera, we need to check whether there is a camera present already. If there is, we stop the old camera. Then, we set up the `viewfinder` class using the `viewfinder` widget, which we did in the **Design** mode. After specifying the capture mode to `CaptureStillImage`, we can start the camera.

 The camera cannot start again if it's not deallocated (stopped).

Consequently, it goes to the `onCaptureButtonClicked` slot. Similarly, the `imgCapture` object is constructed by passing the `camera` and `this` arguments as its `QCamera` target and `QObject` parent respectively. Then, we have to connect the `imageCaptured` signal to the `onImageCaptured` slot of `MainWindow`. Now, let `camera->searchAndLock()` lock all the camera settings. This function is in response to the shutter button being half pressed. Before taking a shot, we set the capture destination to the file. Although it can be set to a buffer using the `QCameraImageCapture::CaptureToBuffer` flag if needed, bear in mind that it's not supported on all platforms.

If everything goes well, an image will be captured by `camera` and the `imageCaptured` signal will be emitted. Then, the `onImageCaptured` slot function will be executed. Inside this function, we scale the captured image to the size of our `previewLabel`. Then, just set `QPixmap` for `previewLabel` and unlock `camera`. In the end, we call the `deleteLater()` function to safely delete the `imgCapture` instance.

 You should explicitly indicate `Qt::KeepAspectRatio`, otherwise it uses the default `Qt::IgnoreAspectRatio` flag.

Now, run the demo and see what you get.

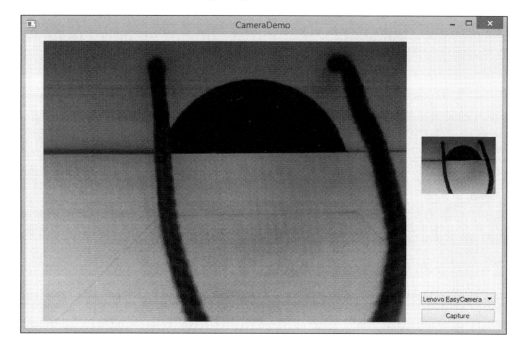

Just as we did in the previous chapters, feel free to change the window's title, application font, and so on. These trivial tweaks won't be detailed anymore.

Controlling the camera

The QCameraFocus class is mentioned to control the zoom and focus of the camera. Speaking of zoom, Qt supports both optical and digital zoom. As we all know, optical zoom offers a better quality than digital. Hence, optical zoom should take priority over digital.

Drag a horizontal slider and a label to **MainWindow** pane's verticalLayout just above the capture button. Name them zoomSlider and zoomLabel, respectively. Remember to change the text of zoomLabel to Zoom and Horizontal in alignment to AlignHCenter. Since Qt doesn't provide a floating point number slider, we simply multiply 10 to get an integer in the slider. Hence, change the minimum value of zoomSlider to 10, which means zoom by 1.0.

Include QCameraFocus in mainwindow.h and add these two private members:

```
QCameraFocus *cameraFocus;
qreal maximumOptZoom;
```

 Not every camera supports zoom. If it doesn't, the maximum zoom is 1.0, which applies to both optical and digital zoom.

There is a type named qreal, which is basically a double value. It was float on the ARM platforms for performance concerns and double on others. However, Qt has used double on ARM by default since the Qt 5.2 version. Anyway, using qreal is recommended if the application is deployed on different hardware platforms.

A new slot also needs to be declared:

```
void onZoomChanged(int);
```

Now, connect zoomSlider in the MainWindow class' constructor:

```
connect(ui->zoomSlider, &QSlider::valueChanged, this,
    &MainWindow::onZoomChanged);
```

However, QCameraFocus can't be constructed explicitly. Instead, it can only be retrieved from the QCamera class. So, we get cameraFocus just after the construction of the camera argument inside onCameraChanged:

```
cameraFocus = camera->focus();
```

Then, set up `maximumOptZoom` and the `maximum` value of `zoomSlider`:

```
maximumOptZoom = cameraFocus->maximumOpticalZoom();
ui->zoomSlider->setMaximum(maximumOptZoom * cameraFocus->
  maximumDigitalZoom() * 10);
```

If the camera doesn't support zoom at all, the slider won't be able to slide. The definition of the `onZoomChanged` slot is shown in the following lines:

```
void MainWindow::onZoomChanged(int z)
{
  qreal zoom = qreal(z) / 10.0;
  if (zoom > maximumOptZoom) {
    cameraFocus->zoomTo(maximumOptZoom, zoom / maximumOptZoom);
  }
  else {
    cameraFocus->zoomTo(zoom, 1.0);
  }
}
```

As you can see, the first parameter of `zoomTo` is the optical zoom factor while the other is the digital zoom factor.

Displaying errors on the status bar

First of all, there could be errors during the whole camera process and it's a good practice to make the user aware of what the error is. It can be done by a pop-up dialog and/or status bar. You don't want to alert the user to every trivial error. Therefore, it'd be better to use a pop-up dialog only for critical errors, while displaying non-critical errors and warnings on the status bar.

Qt began supporting the status bar a long time ago. The `QStatusBar` class is the one that provides a horizontal bar suitable for presenting status information. The status of the camera can be displayed as well and it'll be introduced in later topics.

To use the status bar, edit `mainwindow.ui`, right-click on `MainWindow`, and select **Create Status Bar** if it doesn't exist or was previously removed.

Then, we should declare two slots to handle the camera and image capture errors, respectively. Add these two lines to `private slots` in `mainwindow.h`:

```
void onCameraError();
void onImageCaptureError(int, QCameraImageCapture::Error, const
  QString &);
```

The definitions in `mainwindow.cpp` are shown as follows:

```
void MainWindow::onCameraError()
{
  ui->statusBar->showMessage(camera->errorString(), 5000);
}

void MainWindow::onImageCaptureError(int,
  QCameraImageCapture::Error, const QString &err)
{
  ui->statusBar->showMessage(err, 5000);
  imgCapture->deleteLater();
}
```

This simply makes `statusBar` show a temporary message for five seconds. Even if you pass zero to `showMessage`, it's still a temporary message. In later cases, it won't disappear after a given period; instead, it'll disappear if there is a new temporary message.

Since the signal error is different in `QCamera` from `QCameraImageCapture`, we use different slots to handle it. For `QCamera`, the `error` signal function has `QCamera::Error` as the only argument.

By contrast, `QCameraImageCapture::error` provides three arguments: `int`, `QCameraImageCapture::Error`, and a `const QString` reference. Therefore, we can make use of this signal by using its error `string` directly.

Don't forget to connect the signals and slots. Here, inside the `onCameraChanged` function, just after the `camera` construction, connect the `camera` error and the `onCameraError` slot.

```
connect(camera, static_cast<void (QCamera::*)
  (QCamera::Error)>(&QCamera::error), this,
    &MainWindow::onCameraError);
```

As there is another overloaded function called `error` in the `QCamera` class, we have to use `static_cast` to specify the signal function, as we did in `QComboBox`.

Similarly, add the `connect` statement after the `imgCapture` object's construction in the `onCaptureButtonClicked` function.

```
connect(imgCapture, static_cast<void (QCameraImageCapture::*)
  (int, QCameraImageCapture::Error, const QString
    &)>(&QCameraImageCapture::error), this,
      &MainWindow::onImageCaptureError);
```

It is another overloaded `error` signal function. However, it's tedious because of three arguments.

Permanent widgets in the status bar

Sometimes, we want a sort of indicator inside the status bar to display real-time status, such as the camera status. This is inappropriate if it's covered by temporary messages. In such a case, QStatusBar provides the insertPermanentWidget function to add a widget to the status bar permanently. It means that it won't be obscured by temporary messages and is located on the far right of the status bar.

Firstly, let's make a camera status widget. Add a new C++ class named CameraStatusWidget that inherits from QWidget, but use QLabel as the base class. We use QLabel as the base class because the status of the camera is displayed in text and is basically a customized label widget. The camerastatuswidget.h content is shown as follows:

```cpp
#ifndef CAMERASTATUSWIDGET_H
#define CAMERASTATUSWIDGET_H

#include <QLabel>
#include <QCamera>

class CameraStatusWidget : public QLabel
{
  Q_OBJECT
  public:
    explicit CameraStatusWidget(QWidget *parent = 0);

  public slots:
    void onCameraStatusChanged(QCamera::Status);
};

#endif // CAMERASTATUSWIDGET_H
```

Besides the #include <QCamera>, we only add a declaration of the onCameraStatusChanged slot to this header file. The relevant camerastatuswidget. cpp source file is pasted as follows:

```cpp
#include "camerastatuswidget.h"

CameraStatusWidget::CameraStatusWidget(QWidget *parent) :
  QLabel(parent)
{
}
```

```
void CameraStatusWidget::onCameraStatusChanged(QCamera::Status s)
{
  QString status;
  switch (s) {
    case QCamera::ActiveStatus:
      status = QString("Active");
      break;
    case QCamera::StartingStatus:
      status = QString("Starting");
      break;
    case QCamera::StoppingStatus:
      status = QString("Stopping");
      break;
    case QCamera::StandbyStatus:
      status = QString("Standby");
      break;
    case QCamera::LoadedStatus:
      status = QString("Loaded");
      break;
    case QCamera::LoadingStatus:
      status = QString("Loading");
      break;
    case QCamera::UnloadingStatus:
      status = QString("Unloading");
      break;
    case QCamera::UnloadedStatus:
      status = QString("Unloaded");
      break;
    case QCamera::UnavailableStatus:
      status = QString("Unavailable");
      break;
    default:
      status = QString("Unknown");
  }
  this->setText(status);
}
```

 Always handle exceptions in the switch statements.

QCamera::Status is an enum type. That's why we have to use a switch statement to translate the status to string. Since we have our camera status widget now, it's time to add it to the status bar. Edit mainwindow.h and add a CameraStatusWidget pointer as follows:

```
CameraStatusWidget *camStatusWid;
```

Don't forget to include the camerastatuswidget.h header file. Then, set up camStatusWid just after ui->setupUi(this) by adding the following lines:

```
camStatusWid = new CameraStatusWidget(ui->statusBar);
ui->statusBar->addPermanentWidget(camStatusWid);
```

Navigate to the onCameraChanged function; we need to connect the QCamera::statusChanged signal. Just add the following line after construction of the camera:

```
connect(camera, &QCamera::statusChanged, camStatusWid,
    &CameraStatusWidget::onCameraStatusChanged);
```

Likewise, we can add current zoom to the status bar. In fact, for this small and easy-to-do widget, we don't need to create a new class. Instead, we'll use the existing QLabel class to achieve this by declaring a new member. In mainwindow.h, add a new private member:

```
QLabel *zoomStatus;
```

Meanwhile, construct and insert the zoomStatus into statusBar in the MainWindow class constructor in mainwindow.cpp:

```
zoomStatus = new QLabel(QString::number(qreal(ui->zoomSlider-
    >value()) / 10.0), this);
ui->statusBar->addPermanentWidget(zoomStatus);
```

Here, we use a number function, which is a static public function of the QString class to convert a number (it can be double or integer) to QString. In order to update zoomStatus in time, append this line to the onZoomChanged function:

```
zoomStatus->setText(QString::number(zoom));
```

After these modifications, the application will run as shown in the following screenshot:

Utilizing the menu bar

Now that you have finished the bar at the bottom, it's time to begin the one on top—the menu bar. Similar to the status bar, right-click on MainWindow in the **Design** mode, and select **Create Menu Bar** if it doesn't exist or was previously removed.

Then, just follow the hints. Add a **File** menu containing the **Exit** action. Another menu could be **About**, which contains the **About CameraDemo** action. You should know that these actions are able to change in the **Action Editor** panel, which is in the same place as **Signals & Slots Editor**.

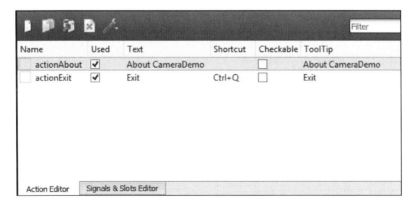

As shown in the following screenshot, the names of these actions are changed to `actionAbout` and `actionExit`, respectively. In addition to this, there is a shortcut, *Ctrl + Q,* for `actionExit`. Just double-click on the action and add shortcuts by pressing the shortcut you want. This is shown in the following screenshot:

We already used `QMenu` and `QAction` in *Chapter 2, Building a Beautiful Cross-platform Clock*. The difference here is that you use `QMenu` as the menu bar, and set it up it in **Design** mode instead of writing code. But why is it called `QAction`? This is because the user can trigger a command on the menu, tool bar, or keyboard shortcut. They expect the same behavior regardless of where it is. Therefore, it should be abstracted into an action, which can be inserted into the menu or tool bar. You can set it to the checkable `QAction` option and use it as a simple `QCheckbox` option.

Let's finish `actionExit` first, since it's simpler than the other one. For `actionExit`, we only need one `connect` statement to make it work. Add the following statement to the `MainWindow` class constructor in the `mainwindow.cpp` file:

```
connect(ui->actionExit, &QAction::triggered, this,
    &MainWindow::close);
```

The `triggered` signal will be emitted by either a mouse click or a keyboard shortcut (if there is a shortcut). Since we connect it to the `close` slot of `MainWindow`, it'll close `MainWindow`, which results in exiting the entire application.

Meanwhile, we need to declare a slot to fulfill the connection with `actionAbout`. As usual, declare it in the `mainwindow.h` header file.

```
void onAboutTriggered();
```

You may think that we're going to create a new class just to show an **About** dialog. Well, we don't have to cook the **About** dialog ourselves because Qt has already done this for us. It's included in QMessageBox, so you should include it with the following line:

```
#include <QMessageBox>
```

This is the definition of the slot:

```
void MainWindow::onAboutTriggered()
{
    QMessageBox::about(this, QString("About"), QString("Camera
        Demonstration of Qt5"));
}
```

 The QMessageBox class provides a modal dialog for informing or asking the user a question and receiving an answer.

Almost every kind of pop-up dialog can be found in QMessageBox. Here, we use the static About function to create an **About** dialog. It has three arguments. The first one is the parent QObject pointer, followed by the title and context. Remember to connect the signal and slot in the MainWindow class constructor.

```
connect(ui->actionAbout, &QAction::triggered, this,
    &MainWindow::onAboutTriggered);
```

If you compile and run the application again, try to trigger the **About** dialog, which would look similar to the following screenshot:

 In addition to About, there are other useful static public members of QMessageBox. Most commonly, critical, information, question, and, warning are used to pop up a message box. Sometimes, you'll see an **About Qt** entry in the menu bar, which is to call the aboutQt function.

In fact, the **About** dialog will display an icon if it exists. There is an empty space since it lacks an icon. The order of the search icons is shown as follows:

- This first icon will be `parent->icon()`, if it exists.
- The second icon will be the top-level widget, which contains `parent`.
- The third icon will be the active window.
- The fourth icon will be the `Information` icon.

Using QFileDialog

The last step of taking a photo is to save it to disk. At this point, the program saves an image to the file, but the location is determined by the camera backend. We can simply use a dialog, letting the user choose the directory and the filename of the photo. There is a `QFileDialog` class to help make the work easier. The easiest way to create a `QFileDialog` class is to use the static functions. Therefore, edit the `onCaptureButtonClicked` function in the `mainwindow.cpp` file.

```
void MainWindow::onCaptureButtonClicked()
{
    imgCapture = new QCameraImageCapture(camera, this);
    connect(imgCapture, static_cast<void (QCameraImageCapture::*)
        (int, QCameraImageCapture::Error, const QString
          &)>(&QCameraImageCapture::error), this,
            &MainWindow::onImageCaptureError);
    connect(imgCapture, &QCameraImageCapture::imageCaptured, this,
        &MainWindow::onImageCaptured);

    camera->searchAndLock();
    imgCapture->setCaptureDestination
        (QCameraImageCapture::CaptureToFile);
    QString location = QFileDialog::getSaveFileName(this,
        QString("Save Photo As"), QString(), "JPEG Image (*.jpg)");
    imgCapture->capture(location);
}
```

Here, we're using the `getSaveFileName` static function to create a file dialog to return the file that the user selected. If the user clicks on **Cancel**, the `location` type would be an empty `QString` reference and the image will be stored in a default location. The file doesn't need to exist. In fact, if it exists, there will be an overwrite dialog. This function's prototype is pasted as follows:

```
QString QFileDialog::getSaveFileName(QWidget * parent = 0, const
  QString & caption = QString(), const QString & dir = QString(),
    const QString & filter = QString(), QString * selectedFilter =
      0, Options options = 0)
```

The first argument is the QObject parent, as usual. The second one is the dialog's title, followed by the default directory. The filter object is used to restrict the file type and it's possible to use multiple filters that are separated by two semicolons, ;;. Here is an example:

```
"JPEG (*.jpeg *.jpg);;PNG (*.png);;BMP (*.bmp)"
```

Setting selectedFilter can change the default filter. Lastly, Options is used to define the behaviors of the file dialog. For more details, refer to the QFileDialog documentation.

QML camera

So far, we talked about how to access and control the camera in Qt/C++. Now it's time to see how QML does in this area. Although there are some limitations, you'll find it's much easier and more elegant to do this in Qt Quick/QML because of the many packages that Qt has to offer.

Create a new Qt Quick application project. The main.qml content is shown as follows:

```
import QtQuick 2.3
import QtQuick.Controls 1.2
import QtMultimedia 5.3
import "qrc:/"

ApplicationWindow {
  visible: true
  width: 640
  height: 480
  title: qsTr("QML Camera Demo")

  Camera {
    id: camera

    imageCapture {
      onImageCaptured: {
```

```
                photoPreview.source = preview
                photoPreview.visible = true;
                previewTimer.running = true;
            }
        }
    }

    VideoOutput {
        id: viewfinder
        source: camera
        anchors.fill: parent
    }

    Image {
        id: photoPreview
        anchors.fill: viewfinder
    }

    Timer {
        id: previewTimer
        interval: 2000
        onTriggered: photoPreview.visible = false;
    }

    CaptureButton {
        anchors.right: parent.right
        anchors.verticalCenter: parent.verticalCenter
        diameter: 50
    }
}
```

Let me walk you through this one.

`Camera` and `VideoOutput` are provided by the `QtMultimedia` module. Similar
to the Qt/C++ classes, the `Camera` type is identical to the `QCamera` class. The
preview is dealt with differently when `VideoOutput` is used as `viewfinder`.
An `image` object is used to display the captured photo and it's only visible for 2
seconds each time a picture is taken. This `photoPreview` is controlled by the timer,
`previewTimer`. In other words, the 2 seconds show up of `photoPreview` depends
on this `previewTimer` timer. At the same time, the `camera` type's `imageCapture` will
provide the `preview` image to `photoPreview` and turn on `previewTimer` once it
captures a photo.

The last piece is `CaptureButton`, which is not provided by Qt but written in another
file, `CaptureButton.qml`. Its content is shown in the following code:

```
import QtQuick 2.3

Rectangle {
  property real diameter

  width: diameter
  height: diameter

  color: "blue"
  border.color: "grey"
  border.width: diameter / 5
  radius: diameter * 0.5

  MouseArea {
    anchors.fill: parent
    onClicked: camera.imageCapture.capture()
  }
}
```

Since there is no circular shape provided by Qt Quick, we use this Rectangle object as a workaround to display it as a circle. Just like what we did in the previous chapter, define a diameter property to hold both height and width. The trick is the radius value. By setting it to half the diameter, this Rectangle object becomes circular. Last but not least, add MouseArea to respond to a user's click. It's a pity that MouseArea can't be circular, so just leave it and fill in the button.

Now you can run your application, and it should be something similar to this:

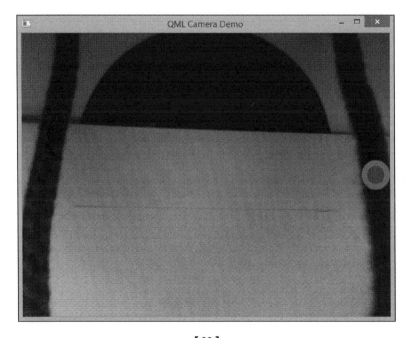

It's not as powerful as the Qt/C++ demo. The first thing you probably notice is that you can't change the camera device. It's missing in the current version of Qt, but it should be supported in the future. In the meantime, the only solution to this is to write a C++ plugin while the main part is still written in QML. Since developing a C++ plugin for QML will be covered in a later chapter, we'll simply skip this part here.

We can make the file dialog in QML in an even more elegant way. Qt Quick provides commonly-used dialogs through the QtQuick.Dialogs module. Therefore, first import this module:

```
import QtQuick.Dialogs 1.2
```

What're we interested in is the FileDialog type, which provides a basic file chooser. It allows the user to select existing files and/or directories, or create new filenames. It uses the native platform file dialogs wherever possible. To use this type, add FileDialog inside ApplicationWindow in the main.qml file.

```
FileDialog {
  id: saveDlg
  property string location

  title: "Save Photo As"
  selectExisting: false
  nameFilters: [ "JPEG (*.jpg)" ]
  onAccepted: {
    location = saveDlg.fileUrl
    camera.imageCapture.captureToLocation(location.slice(8))
  }
}
```

The string type in QML is an extended version of the JavaScript string type. Wherever possible, you should avoid the var keyword and use the exact type, such as int, double, and string. According to the QML documentation, this will improve performance since the machine doesn't need to guess the data type. Here, we declare location, which is a string type, while the rest of its properties are similar to the dialog settings in Qt/C++, its title (caption), and nameFilters. You should set the selectExisting property to false, as it is true by default. Otherwise, it'll behave like an open file dialog.

Inside the `onAccepted` handler, pass the `fileUrl` value to `location` first. This handler is the response to the `accepted` signal, which is emitted if the user selects a file successfully. The `fileUrl` property will then be changed. It's in a URI format, which has an extra `file:///` prefix. In addition to this, there is currently an issue if we execute `slice` on `fileUrl` directly. So as a workaround, we use the explicitly declared `string location` to invoke the `slice` function. This is a JavaScript function, which will return a new `string` type that contains the extracted parts of a string. The `slice` method's prototype is `slice(start,end)` where `end` will be the end of the `string` type if it's omitted. Also, note that the character at the `start` position is included and the index starts from zero. After that, we simply call the `captureToLocation` function of `imageCapture` to store the image at the selected location.

In order to make it work, we have to change the behavior of `CaptureButton`. Edit the `CaptureButton.qml` file and change `MouseArea`, as shown in the following lines:

```
MouseArea {
    anchors.fill: parent
    onClicked: saveDlg.open()
    onPressed: parent.color = "black"
    onReleased: parent.color = "blue"
}
```

In addition to this, to change the `onClicked` handler, we also add `onPressed` and `onReleased` to let it have the push effect. As you can see, the `open()` function will execute our `FileDialog`. On a desktop operating system, such as Windows, the platform file dialog is used as shown here:

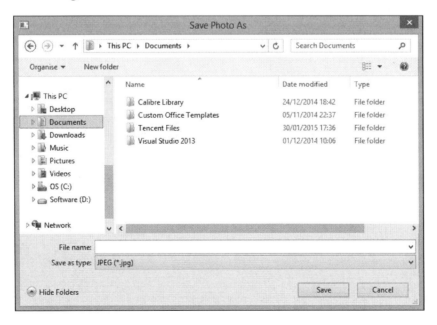

The inner circle of `CaptureButton` will become black once it's pressed, and then go back to blue when the mouse is released. Although it's just a minor visual effect, it definitely improves the user experience.

"Do not fail to commit an act of kindness just because it is small in scale."

To complete this QML camera application, we need to add a zoom control as we did for the Qt/C++ camera. Add a new QML file named `ZoomControl.qml`, whose content is shown as follows:

```
import QtQuick 2.3

Item {
  property real zoom: camera.opticalZoom * camera.digitalZoom

  function zoomControl() {
    if (zoom > camera.maximumOpticalZoom) {
      camera.digitalZoom = zoom / camera.maximumOpticalZoom
      camera.opticalZoom = camera.maximumOpticalZoom
    }
    else {
      camera.digitalZoom = 1.0
      camera.opticalZoom = zoom
    }
  }

  Text {
    id: indicator
    anchors.fill: parent
    horizontalAlignment: Text.AlignHCenter
    verticalAlignment: Text.AlignVCenter
    color: "darkgrey"
    font.bold: true
    font.family: "Segoe"
    font.pointSize: 20
    style: Text.Raised
    styleColor: "black"
  }

  Timer {
    id: indicatorTimer
    interval: 2000
    onTriggered: indicator.visible = false
  }
```

```
MouseArea {
  anchors.fill: parent
  onWheel: {
    if (wheel.angleDelta.y > 0) {
      zoom += 1.0
      if (zoom > camera.maximumOpticalZoom *
        camera.maximumOpticalZoom) {
        zoom -= 1.0
      }
      else {
        zoomControl()
      }
    }
    else {
      zoom -= 1.0
      if (zoom < camera.maximumOpticalZoom *
        camera.maximumOpticalZoom) {
        zoom += 1.0
      }
      else {
        zoomControl()
      }
    }
    indicator.text = "X " + zoom.toString()
    indicator.visible = true
    indicatorTimer.running = true
  }
}
}
```

First, we declare `property` of the `real` type to store the current zoom, whose initial value is the camera's current zoom, which is itself the multiplication of the current digital and optical zoom. This is followed by a JavaScript-style function, `zoomControl`. As mentioned before, you can use JavaScript in QML anywhere seamlessly. This function is identical to the Qt/C++ slot, `onZoomChanged`, in the previous topic.

Then, there is a `Text` element used to display the current `zoom` function on screen. These are just some visual customizations inside the `Text` element, which include centering in the parent by setting both the horizontal and vertical alignments.

What's next is a `Timer` element that controls the visibility of `Text`, similar to the controller of `photoPreview`.

The last but also the trickiest is `MouseArea`. We use the mouse wheel to control the zoom, so the handler that can get the wheel event is `onWheel`. The `wheel.angleDelta.y` is the wheel, which is rotated to a vertical orientation. If it's positive, it goes up; otherwise, it goes down. It zooms in with a positive value, and zooms out with negative one. You have to ensure that the new zoom is within the supported zoom range of `camera` before invoking the `zoomControl` function. After this, let the `Text` indicator display `zoom` and turn on `Timer` so that it's only visible for 2 seconds. You can also see that there is a built-in function for the `real` element to convert it to `string`, just like the `QString::number` function in Qt/C++.

After all this, edit `main.qml` and add `ZoomControl` to the application, as shown in the following code:

```
ZoomControl {
    anchors.fill: viewfinder
}
```

Be aware that `ZoomControl` should fill in `viewfinder` instead of `parent`; otherwise, it may get overlaid by other components, such as `viewfinder`.

Give this QML camera a test run and compare which one is better.

Summary

By the end of this chapter, you should be able to write applications that can access camera devices in either Qt/C++ or QML. What's more is that you should be able to utilize the status and menu bar in traditional desktop applications, which are historically important and continue to play a crucial role as interactive functional widgets. In addition to this, don't forget the file dialog and message box since they make your coding work easier. In the next chapter, we're going to talk about an advanced topic, plugins, which is a popular way to extend large applications.

5

Extending Paint Applications with Plugins

Plugins enable you to make your application extendable and friendly for other developers. Therefore, in this chapter, we'll guide you in how to write plugins for Qt applications. A paint application demonstrates the recipe for Qt/C++. A simple demonstration shows you how to write a C++ plugin for QML. The topics we will cover in this chapter are listed as follows:

- Drawing via QPainter
- Writing static plugins
- Writing dynamic plugins
- Merging plugin and main program projects
- Creating a C++ plugins for QML applications

Drawing via QPainter

Before we get started, let me introduce the QPainter class to you. This class performs low-level painting on widgets and other paint devices. In fact, everything drawn on the screen in a Qt application is the result of QPainter. It can draw almost anything, including simple lines and aligned text. Thanks to the high-level APIs that Qt has provided, it's extremely easy to use these rich features.

Qt's paint system consists of QPainter, QPaintDevice, and QPaintEngine. In this chapter, we won't need to deal with the latter two. The relations diagram is sketched as follows:

QPainter is used to perform drawing operations, while QPaintDevice is an abstraction of a two-dimensional space that can be painted on by using QPainter. QPaintEngine provides the interface that the painter uses to draw onto different types of devices. Note that the QPaintEngine class is used internally by QPainter and QPaintDevice. It's also designed to be hidden from programmers unless they create their own device type.

So basically, what we need to concentrate on is QPainter. Let's create a new project and do some exercises in it. The new painter_demo project is a Qt Widget application. Quickly create it and add a new C++ Canvas class that inherits from QWidget. Canvas is our customized widget whose header file is shown as follows:

```cpp
#ifndef CANVAS_H
#define CANVAS_H

#include <QWidget>

class Canvas : public QWidget
{
  Q_OBJECT
  public:
    explicit Canvas(QWidget *parent = 0);

  private:
    QVector<QPointF> m_points;

  protected:
    void paintEvent(QPaintEvent *);
    void mousePressEvent(QMouseEvent *);
    void mouseMoveEvent(QMouseEvent *);
    void mouseReleaseEvent(QMouseEvent *);
};

#endif // CANVAS_H
```

The QVector class is a template class that provides a fast and dynamic array. It's fast because the items are stored in adjacent memory locations, which means that the indexing time is constant. Here, we store the QPointF elements in m_points, where QPointF is a class that defines a point using a floating point precision.

In a protected scope, there are four event functions. We're familiar with these mouse events. The leading one, which is also the new one, is the paintEvent function. Since we're painting on the widget, QPainter should only be used inside the paintEvent function.

The definitions of the functions in canvas.cpp are shown as follows:

```cpp
#include <QStyleOption>
#include <QPainter>
#include <QPaintEvent>
#include <QMouseEvent>
#include "canvas.h"

Canvas::Canvas(QWidget *parent) :
  QWidget(parent)
{
}

void Canvas::paintEvent(QPaintEvent *)
{
  QPainter painter(this);

  QStyleOption opt;
  opt.initFrom(this);
  this->style()->drawPrimitive(QStyle::PE_Widget, &opt, &painter,
    this);

  painter.setPen(QColor(Qt::black));
  painter.setRenderHint(QPainter::Antialiasing);
  painter.drawPolyline(m_points.data(), m_points.count());
}

void Canvas::mousePressEvent(QMouseEvent *e)
{
  m_points.clear();
  m_points.append(e->localPos());
  this->update();
}
```

```
void Canvas::mouseMoveEvent(QMouseEvent *e)
{
  m_points.append(e->localPos());
  this->update();
}

void Canvas::mouseReleaseEvent(QMouseEvent *e)
{
  m_points.append(e->localPos());
  this->update();
}
```

First, let's check what's inside the paintEvent function. The first clause is to initialize a QPainter object, which uses this as QPaintDevice. Well, there is an alternate way to initialize a QPainter class, which is demonstrated here:

```
QPainter painter;
painter.begin(this);
painter.drawPolyline(m_points.data(), m_points.count());
painter.end();
```

If you use the method shown in the preceding code, remember to call the end() function to destroy painter. By contrast, if you initialize QPainter by its constructor, the destructor will automatically call the end() function. However, the constructor won't return a value indicating whether it was initialized successfully or not. Thus, it'd be better to choose the latter method when dealing with an external QPaintDevice such as a printer.

After the initialization, we use QStyleOption, which contains all the information that the QStyle functions need to draw a graphical element and make our customized widget style-aware. We simply use the initFrom function to get the style information. Then, we get the QStyle function of our widget and draw QStyle::PE_Widget with painter using the style options specified by opt. If we don't write these three lines, we can't change the widget display style, such as the background color.

Then, we let the painter use a black pen to draw an anti-aliasing polyline on the widget. Here, an overloaded setPen function is used. The painter.setPen(QColor(Qt::black)) function will set a solid-line style pen with a width of 1 and the color in black. The painter.setRenderHint(QPainter::Antialiasing) function will make the drawing smooth.

A second argument, `bool`, controls the render hint. It's `true` by default, which means that you need to turn on the render hint. You can turn off a render hint by passing a `false` value, though.

A list of the available render hints are shown as follows:

```
QPainter::Antialiasing
QPainter::TextAntialiasing
QPainter::SmoothPixmapTransform
QPainter::Qt4CompatiblePainting
```

There are also two obsolete hints: `QPainter::HighQualityAntialiasing` and `QPainter::NonCosmeticDefaultPen`. The first one is replaced by `QPainter::Antialiasing` and the second is useless because `QPen` is non-cosmetic by default now.

Finally, the `drawPolyline` function will draw a polyline, which is made from the mouse movements, on the `Canvas` widget. The first argument is the pointer to a `QPointF` or `QPoint` array, while the second one is the number of items inside that array.

Speaking of mouse movements, three mouse event functions are used to track the mouse. In fact, they're pretty self-explanatory. When a mouse press event occurs, purge the points array because it's obviously a new polyline now, and then add the mouse position by invoking a `localPos()` function. The `localPos()` function will return the position of the mouse relative to the widget or item that received the event. Although you can get a global position by the `screenPos()` and `globalPos()` function, in most cases, we only need a local position. At the end of these event functions, call `update()` to repaint the widget to show the mouse moving path as a polyline.

Now, edit `mainwindow.ui` in the **Design** mode. Remove the status bar since we won't use it in this chapter, but keep the menu bar. Drag **Widget** to `centralWidget` and rename it as `canvas`. Right-click on `canvas` and select **Promote to ...**, and then fill in `Canvas` in **Promoted class name**. Now, click on **Add**, and then on **Promote**. You shouldn't check the **Global include** box because the `canvas.h` header file is in our project directory instead of the global include directory.

Inside **Property**, edit `styleSheet`, input `background-color: rgb(255, 255, 255);` so that the canvas has a white background. Then, change the `MainWindow` class' layout to **Lay Out Horizontally** or **Lay Out Vertically** so that the `canvas` widget can fill the whole frame. Give your application a run now; you should expect a simple white painter as follows:

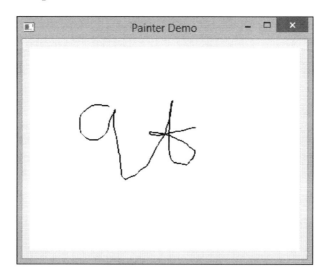

This painter is too simple to hold the old lines. While Qt doesn't provide an API to paint on the old scene, `QImage` can get us out of this dilemma. In other words, when the mouse moves, we paint a stroke on a `QImage` object, and then paint this `QImage` object onto `Canvas`.

The new header file, `canvas.h`, is as shown as follows:

```
#ifndef CANVAS_H
#define CANVAS_H

#include <QWidget>

class Canvas : public QWidget
{
  Q_OBJECT
  public:
    explicit Canvas(QWidget *parent = 0);

  private:
    QVector<QPointF> m_points;
    QImage image;
```

```
    void updateImage();

  protected:
    void paintEvent(QPaintEvent *);
    void mousePressEvent(QMouseEvent *);
    void mouseMoveEvent(QMouseEvent *);
    void mouseReleaseEvent(QMouseEvent *);
    void resizeEvent(QResizeEvent *);
};

#endif // CANVAS_H
```

The differences include the declaration of a `QImage` object, `image`; private member function, `updateImage()`; and a reimplemented function, `resizeEvent(QResizeEvent *)`. The `paintEvent(QPaintEvent *)` function is also changed to draw the `image` object instead, whereas there are more modifications in the `canvas.cpp` source file than the header file, whose content is shown here:

```
#include <QStyleOption>
#include <QPainter>
#include <QPaintEvent>
#include <QMouseEvent>
#include <QResizeEvent>
#include "canvas.h"

Canvas::Canvas(QWidget *parent) :
  QWidget(parent)
{
}

void Canvas::paintEvent(QPaintEvent *e)
{
  QPainter painter(this);

  QStyleOption opt;
  opt.initFrom(this);
  this->style()->drawPrimitive(QStyle::PE_Widget, &opt, &painter,
    this);

  painter.drawImage(e->rect().topLeft(), image);
}

void Canvas::updateImage()
{
```

```cpp
    QPainter painter(&image);
    painter.setPen(QColor(Qt::black));
    painter.setRenderHint(QPainter::Antialiasing);
    painter.drawPolyline(m_points.data(), m_points.count());
    this->update();
}

void Canvas::mousePressEvent(QMouseEvent *e)
{
    m_points.clear();
    m_points.append(e->localPos());
    updateImage();
}

void Canvas::mouseMoveEvent(QMouseEvent *e)
{
    m_points.append(e->localPos());
    updateImage();
}

void Canvas::mouseReleaseEvent(QMouseEvent *e)
{
    m_points.append(e->localPos());
    updateImage();
}

void Canvas::resizeEvent(QResizeEvent *e)
{
    QImage newImage(e->size(), QImage::Format_RGB32);
    newImage.fill(Qt::white);
    QPainter painter(&newImage);
    painter.drawImage(0, 0, image);
    image = newImage;
    QWidget::resizeEvent(e);
}
```

Let's look into the mouse event handlers; after the operation on m_points, the updateImage() function is called instead of update(). Inside the updateImage() function, we create a QPainter object using the QImage object image as QPaintDevice while the rest of them are just the same as in paintEvent.

There is a new member function, though, called `resizeEvent`, which is reimplemented from `QWidget`. As you can imagine, we change the underlying `QImage` object once the widget size changes, which could be as a result of window resizing. Therefore, we simply paint the old image onto the new one. This may cause the loss of a part of the image if the new size is smaller than the previous one. You may wish to add `Scroll Area` to `MainWindow` and make `Canvas` the child widget of `Scroll Area`. You already know how to do that in QML, while it's similar in Qt/C++. Therefore, just take it as an exercise and implement `Scroll Area` for this application.

Writing static plugins

There are two types of plugins: static and dynamic. Static plugins are statically linked to the executables, while the dynamic plugins are loaded at runtime. Dynamic plugins exist as the `.dll` or `.so` files, depending on the platform. Although the static plugins will be built as the `.lib` or `.a` files, they'll be integrated into an executable file when the main program gets compiled.

In this topic, we'll get to know how to write a static plugin to extend the application. Serving as an external plugin, it gains the flexibility to change its internal code while it's only required to keep the interface compatible. It's up to you to decide whether the interface should be maintained in the main program or in different plugins. In this example, we'll put the `interface.h` file in the main program, `painter_demo`. The content of `interface.h` is as follows:

```
#ifndef INTERFACE_H
#define INTERFACE_H

#include <QtPlugin>
#include <QPainterPath>

class InsertInterface
{
  public:
    virtual ~InsertInterface() {}
    virtual QString name() const = 0;
    virtual QPainterPath getObject(QWidget *parent) = 0;
};


#define InsertInterface_iid "org.qt-project.Qt.PainterDemo.
InsertInterface"
Q_DECLARE_INTERFACE(InsertInterface, InsertInterface_iid)

#endif // INTERFACE_H
```

As you can see, we declare a pure virtual class, `InsertInterface`. In order to avoid errors, you have to declare a virtual destructor. Otherwise, the compiler may complain and abort the compilation. The `QPainterPath` class provides a container for common 2D painting operations, including `ellipse` and `text`. Hence, the return type of `getObject` is `QPainterPath`, which can be used directly where the argument, `QWidget`, could be useful if there is a newly created dialog to get any input from the user.

At the end of this file, we declare `InsertInterface` as an interface by the `Q_DECLARE_INTERFACE` macro, where `InsertInterface_iid` is the identifier for the `InsertInterface` class. Note that the identifier must be unique, so it's recommended that you use a Java-style naming rule.

Now, we need to create a new project. Navigate to **Libraries | C++ Library**. Then, as shown in the following screenshot, select **Qt Plugin** for **Type** and keep this project inside the main program project folder for the sake of convenience or any concerns:

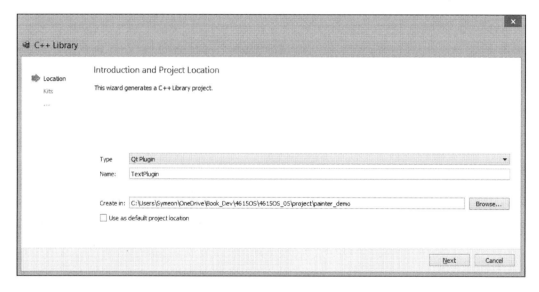

Click on **Next** and choose the same Qt kits as the `painter_demo` project. In this example, the `build` directory is set in the same directory as the `painter_demo` project, which is `D:\Projects\build`. Therefore, the `build` directory of `TextPlugin` is `D:\Projects\build\TextPlugin-Qt_5_4_0_mingw491_32-Debug` and `D:\Projects\build\TextPlugin-Qt_5_4_0_mingw491_32-Release` for `Debug` and `Release`, respectively.

Furthermore, you can change **Default build directory** in
Tools | Options | Build & Run | General. In this book, we
use `D:/Projects/build/%{CurrentProject:Name}-`
`%{CurrentKit:FileSystemName}-%{CurrentBuild:Name}`
so that all the builds are organized in one place.

Then, fill in `TextPlugin` in the `Class name` field, as shown in the following
screenshot:

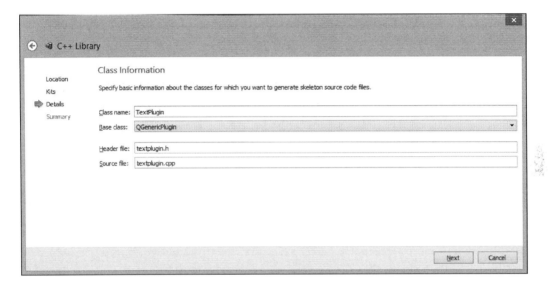

We need to apply some modifications to the `TextPlugin.pro` project file,
as displayed here:

```
QT          += core gui widgets

TARGET = TextPlugin
TEMPLATE = lib
CONFIG += plugin static

DESTDIR = ../plugins

SOURCES += textplugin.cpp

INCLUDEPATH += ../

HEADERS += textplugin.h
OTHER_FILES += TextPlugin.json
```

By adding widgets, we can use some useful classes such as QMessageBox. We also need to add static to CONFIG to declare this a static plugin project. Then, change the DESTDIR variable to ../plugins so that the plugin is installed to the plugins directory outside the build folder. Lastly, we add the upper directory ../ to INCLUDEPATH so that we can include the interface.h header file in this subproject. The textplugin.h file is shown as follows:

```
#ifndef TEXTPLUGIN_H
#define TEXTPLUGIN_H

#include "interface.h"


class TextPlugin : public QObject,
                   public InsertInterface
{
  Q_OBJECT
  Q_PLUGIN_METADATA(IID "org.qt-
    project.Qt.PainterDemo.InsertInterface" FILE
      "TextPlugin.json")
  Q_INTERFACES(InsertInterface)

  public:
    QString name() const;
    QPainterPath getObject(QWidget *parent);
};

#endif // TEXTPLUGIN_H
```

We use the Q_PLUGIN_METADATA macro to specify the unique IID, which is the same as the one we declared in interface.h, where FILE "TextPlugin.json" can be used to contain the metadata for this plugin. In this case, we just keep the TextPlugin.json file intact. Then, the Q_INTERFACES macro tells the compiler that this is a plugin for InsertInterface. In the public scope, there are just two reimplemented functions. Their definitions are located in the textplugin.cpp source file, whose content is pasted as follows:

```
#include <QInputDialog>
#include "textplugin.h"

QString TextPlugin::name() const
{
  return QString("Text");
}
```

```
QPainterPath TextPlugin::getObject(QWidget *parent)
{
  QPainterPath ppath;
  QString text = QInputDialog::getText(parent, QString("Insert
    Text"), QString("Text"));

  if (!text.isEmpty()) {
    ppath.addText(10, 80, QFont("Cambria", 60), text);
  }
  return ppath;
}
```

The `name()` function simply returns the name of this plugin, which is `Text` in this case. As for `getObject`, it constructs a `QPainterPath` class that contains the text given by the user via a pop-up dialog, and then returns the `QPainterPath` object to the main program. The `addText` function will draw the text as a set of closed subpaths created from the font, while the first two arguments define the left end of the baseline for this text.

This is it for the plugin project. Now, just build it and you should expect a `libTextPlugin.a` file to be located under the `plugins` directory, while the `plugins` directory itself should be located in the parent directory of your project's `build` folders, as shown here:

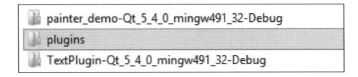

It doesn't matter much if you put the files under other directories, although this means that you need to do some path modifications relevantly afterwards.

Now, let's go back to the main program's project, which is `painter_demo` in this example. Edit its `painter_demo.pro` project file and add the following line to it:

```
LIBS     += -L../plugins -lTextPlugin
```

 The working directory during compilation is the `build` directory instead of the project source code directory.

Then, edit `mainwindow.ui` in the **Design** mode; add a menu named `Plugins` to the menu bar, whose object name is `menuPlugins`.

Among all the changes made in the main program, the modifications for the MainWindow class are maximum. Here is the code of the new `mainwindow.h` file:

```
#ifndef MAINWINDOW_H
#define MAINWINDOW_H

#include <QMainWindow>

namespace Ui {
  class MainWindow;
}

class MainWindow : public QMainWindow
{
  Q_OBJECT

  public:
    explicit MainWindow(QWidget *parent = 0);
    ~MainWindow();

  private:
    Ui::MainWindow *ui;

    void loadPlugins();
    void generatePluginMenu(QObject *);

  private slots:
    void onInsertInterface();
};

#endif // MAINWINDOW_H
```

Still no clue about it? Well, its `mainwindow.cpp` source file is pasted here as well:

```
#include <QPluginLoader>
#include "mainwindow.h"
#include "ui_mainwindow.h"
#include "interface.h"

Q_IMPORT_PLUGIN(TextPlugin)

MainWindow::MainWindow(QWidget *parent) :
  QMainWindow(parent),
  ui(new Ui::MainWindow)
{
```

```
    ui->setupUi(this);
    loadPlugins();
}


MainWindow::~MainWindow()
{
    delete ui;
}

void MainWindow::loadPlugins()
{
    foreach(QObject *plugin, QPluginLoader::staticInstances()) {
        generatePluginMenu(plugin);
    }
}


void MainWindow::generatePluginMenu(QObject *plugin)
{
    InsertInterface *insertInterfacePlugin =
        qobject_cast<InsertInterface *>(plugin);
    if (insertInterfacePlugin) {
        QAction *action = new QAction(insertInterfacePlugin->name(),
            plugin);
        connect(action, &QAction::triggered, this,
            &MainWindow::onInsertInterface);
        ui->menuPlugins->addAction(action);
    }
}


void MainWindow::onInsertInterface()
{
    QAction *action = qobject_cast<QAction *>(sender());
    InsertInterface *insertInterfacePlugin =
        qobject_cast<InsertInterface *>(action->parent());
    const QPainterPath ppath =
        insertInterfacePlugin->getObject(this);
    if (!ppath.isEmpty()) {
        ui->canvas->insertPainterPath(ppath);
    }
}
```

You may have figured out that the Q_IMPORT_PLUGIN macro is used to import the plugin. Yes, it is, but only for static plugins. In the loadPlugins() function, we walked through all the static plugin instances and added them to the menu by invoking the generatePluginMenu function.

Plugins are treated as plain QOjbect objects at first, and then you can use qobject_ cast to convert them to their own classes. The qobject_cast class will return a NULL pointer if it failed. Inside the if statement, there is a trick to use the plugin successfully later. Instead of calling a simplified and overloaded addAction function, we can construct QAction and add it to the menu, because QAction will have the plugin as its QObject parent. Therefore, you can see that we convert its parent to the relevant plugin class in the onInsertInterface function. Inside this function, we call the insertPainterPath function to paint the QPainterPath class returned by the plugin on canvas. Of course, we need to declare and define this function in the Canvas class. Add this statement to the public domain of the canvas.h file:

```
void insertPainterPath(const QPainterPath &);
```

The preceding code's definition in canvas.cpp is as follows:

```
void Canvas::insertPainterPath(const QPainterPath &ppath)
{
  QPainter painter(&image);
  painter.drawPath(ppath);
  this->update();
}
```

The preceding statements should be familiar to you and they're also self-explanatory. Now, build and run this application again; don't forget to change the current active project back to painter_demo by right-clicking on the painter_demo project and selecting **Set "painter_demo" as Active Project**. When it runs, click on **Plugins**, select **Text**, input Plugin!! in the pop-up dialog, and confirm. Then, you'll see the text, **Plugin!!**, painted on the canvas as expected.

The executable's size grows as well because we statically linked our TextPlugin project file to it. In addition to this, you have to rebuild the main program if you changed the plugin. Otherwise, the newly generated plugin won't be linked to the executable as it should.

Writing dynamic plugins

Static plugins provide a convenient way to distribute your applications. However, this always requires a rebuild of the main program. By contrast, dynamic plugins are much more flexible since they're linked dynamically. This means the main project, which is painter_demo in this example, doesn't need to be built with dynamic plugins nor is it required to release its source code. Instead, it only needs to provide an interface and the header file of that interface, and then scan those dynamic plugins at runtime so that they can be loaded.

[Dynamic plugins are commonly seen in complex applications, especially in commercial software such as Adobe Illustrator.]

Similar to the static plugin we just wrote, we need to create a new Qt Plugin project and we'll call it EllipsePlugin this time. Although you can write a new interface along with this plugin, here we will just focus on plugin-related topics. So, we just reuse the InsertInterface class while the ellipseplugin.pro project file is shown as follows:

```
QT          += core gui widgets

TARGET = EllipsePlugin
TEMPLATE = lib
CONFIG += plugin

DESTDIR = ../plugins

SOURCES +=  ellipseplugin.cpp \
            ellipsedialog.cpp

HEADERS +=  ellipseplugin.h \
            ellipsedialog.h
OTHER_FILES += EllipsePlugin.json

INCLUDEPATH += ../

FORMS += ellipsedialog.ui
```

Don't forget to change the DESTDIR and INCLUDEPATH variables in the ellipseplugin.pro file though, they're basically the same as the previous TextPlugin project.

Ignoring the source files, forms, and so on, it's basically the same thing with only the removal of static in CONFIG. The ellipseplugin.h header file is shown as follows:

```
#ifndef ELLIPSEPLUGIN_H
#define ELLIPSEPLUGIN_H

#include "interface.h"


class EllipsePlugin : public QObject,
                      public InsertInterface
{
  Q_OBJECT
  Q_PLUGIN_METADATA(IID "org.qt-
    project.Qt.PainterDemo.InsertInterface" FILE
      "EllipsePlugin.json")
  Q_INTERFACES(InsertInterface)

  public:
    QString name() const;
    QPainterPath getObject(QWidget *parent);

  public slots:
    void onDialogAccepted(qreal x, qreal y, qreal wid, qreal hgt);

  private:
    qreal m_x;
    qreal m_y;
    qreal width;
    qreal height;
};

#endif // ELLIPSEPLUGIN_H
```

As you can see in the preceding code, we declare that this is a plugin using InsertInterface as the same in TextPlugin, whereas the difference is the declaration of an onDialogAccepted slot function and several private variables. Accordingly, the ellipseplugin.cpp file is shown as follows:

```
#include "ellipsedialog.h"
#include "ellipseplugin.h"


QString EllipsePlugin::name() const
{
    return QString("Ellipse");
}

QPainterPath EllipsePlugin::getObject(QWidget *parent)
{
    m_x = 0;
    m_y = 0;
    width = 0;
    height = 0;

    EllipseDialog *dlg = new EllipseDialog(parent);
    connect(dlg, &EllipseDialog::accepted, this,
        &EllipsePlugin::onDialogAccepted);
    dlg->exec();

    QPainterPath ppath;
    ppath.addEllipse(m_x, m_y, width, height);
    return ppath;
}

void EllipsePlugin::onDialogAccepted(qreal x, qreal y, qreal wid,
    qreal hgt)
{
    m_x = x;
    m_y = y;
    width = wid;
    height = hgt;
}
```

There is nothing special about the name() function. By contrast, we use the EllipseDialog custom dialog to get some inputs from the user. Remember to connect all the signals and slots associated with the dialog before executing the exec() function; otherwise, the slots simply won't be connected. Also, note that the exec() function will block the event loop and return only after the dialog closes, which is pretty handy for our purposes because we can use the accepted values, such as m_x and m_y, to add an ellipse to QPainterPath.

As for the EllipseDialog custom dialog itself, it was created by adding a new Qt Designer Form Class via Qt Creator. Since it's used to provide an interface for the user to specify some parameters, we use **Form Layout** in this dialog. Add QLabel and QDoubleSpinBox, as suggested in the following screenshot:

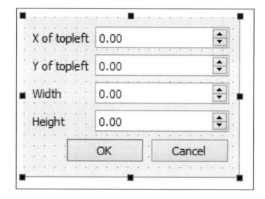

Accordingly, their objectName values are tlXLabel, tlXDoubleSpinBox, tlYLabel, tlYDoubleSpinBox, widthLabel, widthDoubleSpinBox, heightLabel, and heightDoubleSpinBox. You should also change the maximum value to 9999.99 or something big enough in the **Property** panel of QDoubleSpinBox.

In addition to this, also note that there is a removal of the default signal and slot in **Signals & Slots Editor**. Simply delete the accepted() signal pair of buttonBox because we need a more advanced handler. In this form class header file, ellipsedialog.h, we declare a new signal and a new slot:

```
#ifndef ELLIPSEDIALOG_H
#define ELLIPSEDIALOG_H

#include <QDialog>

namespace Ui {
  class EllipseDialog;
}
```

```
class EllipseDialog : public QDialog
{
  Q_OBJECT

  public:
    explicit EllipseDialog(QWidget *parent = 0);
    ~EllipseDialog();

  signals:
    void accepted(qreal, qreal, qreal, qreal);

  private:
    Ui::EllipseDialog *ui;

  private slots:
    void onAccepted();
};


#endif // ELLIPSEDIALOG_H
```

The `accepted(qreal, qreal, qreal, qreal)` signal here passes these values back to the plugin, while the `onAccepted()` slot handles the `accepted()` signal emitted from `buttonBox`. They are defined in the `ellipsedialog.cpp` source file, as shown in the following code:

```
#include "ellipsedialog.h"
#include "ui_ellipsedialog.h"

EllipseDialog::EllipseDialog(QWidget *parent) :
    QDialog(parent),
    ui(new Ui::EllipseDialog)
{
  ui->setupUi(this);

  connect(ui->buttonBox, &QDialogButtonBox::accepted, this,
    &EllipseDialog::onAccepted);
}

EllipseDialog::~EllipseDialog()
{
  delete ui;
}

void EllipseDialog::onAccepted()
{
```

```
        emit accepted(ui->tlXDoubleSpinBox->value(),
          ui->tlYDoubleSpinBox->value(),
            ui->widthDoubleSpinBox->value(),
              ui->heightDoubleSpinBox->value());
        this->accept();
    }
```

Inside the constructor, connect the `accepted()` signal of `buttonBox` to the `onAccepted()` advanced handler slot. In this slot, we emit the `accepted` signal, which contains the values that the user has entered. Then, call the `accept()` function to close this dialog.

`EllipsePlugin` is finished at this point. Click on the **Build** button in the panel to build this project. You should expect the output, `EllipsePlugin.dll` on Windows, to be located in the same `plugins` directory as the previous `TextPlugin` project.

To make use of this dynamic plugin, we need a final step, which is to make the main program load the dynamic plugin(s). What we have to change here is the `loadPlugins()` function in `mainwindow.cpp`:

```
    void MainWindow::loadPlugins()
    {
      foreach(QObject *plugin, QPluginLoader::staticInstances()) {
        generatePluginMenu(plugin);
      }

      //search and load dynamic plugins
      QDir pluginDir = QDir(qApp->applicationDirPath());
      #ifdef Q_OS_WIN
      QString dirName = pluginDir.dirName();
      if (dirName.compare(QString("debug"), Qt::CaseInsensitive) == 0
        || dirName.compare(QString("release"), Qt::CaseInsensitive) ==
          0) {
        pluginDir.cdUp();
        pluginDir.cdUp();
      }
      #endif
      pluginDir.cd(QString("plugins"));

      foreach (QString fileName, pluginDir.entryList(QDir::Files)) {
        QPluginLoader loader(pluginDir.absoluteFilePath(fileName));
        QObject *plugin = loader.instance();
        if (plugin) {
          generatePluginMenu(plugin);
        }
      }
    }
```

In order to use the `QDir` class, you may also need to include this:

```
#include <QDir>
```

The `QDir` class will provide access to directory structures and their contents, which we use to locate our dynamic plugins. The `qApp` macro is a global pointer, referring to this very application instance. It's equivalent to the `QCoreApplication::instance()` function and `QApplication::instance()` for non-GUI and GUI applications, respectively. On Windows platforms, our `plugins` directory is located in the second upper folder of the `build` path.

Then, we just test each file in the `plugins` directory, load it, and generate a proper menu entry if it's a loadable plugin. Run this application again; you'll have an **Ellipse** entry inside the **Plugins** menu. It works as expected.

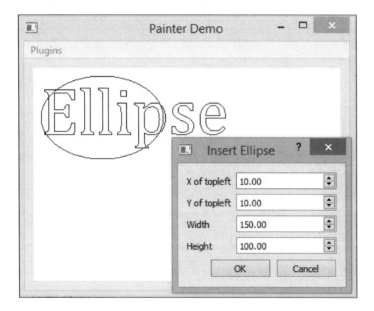

Merging plugins and main program projects

It is a tedious thing that opens several projects and builds them in order. This is not a big deal given that we have just two plugins and a main program. However, it'll become a serious inefficiency issue once the number of plugins increase. Therefore, it is a better practice to merge the plugins into the main project and get them built in a specified order every time we click on the **Build** button. It's totally feasible and is commonly seen in Qt projects.

Firstly, we move all the files in the `painter_demo` directory, except for the `EllipsePlugin` and `TextPlugin` folders, into a newly created `main` folder.

Then, rename the `painter_demo.pro` to `main.pro` in the `main` folder while creating a new `painter_demo.pro` project file outside in the `painter_demo` directory. This new `painter_demo.pro` project file needs to have contents as shown in the following code:

```
TEMPLATE   = subdirs
CONFIG    += ordered
SUBDIRS    = TextPlugin \
             EllipsePlugin \
             main
```

The `subdirs` project is a special template, which means that this project file won't generate an application or a library. Instead, it tells qmake to build subdirectories. By adding `ordered` to `CONFIG`, we can ensure that the compiling process follows the exact order according to `SUBDIRS`.

To accomplish this, we need to modify the project files in the two plugins directories. Change the `INCLUDEPATH` variable to the following line:

```
INCLUDEPATH += ../main
```

This change is obvious because we moved all the source code into the `main` directory. If we don't change `INCLUDEPATH`, the compiler will complain that it can't find the `interface.h` header file.

Creating a C++ plugin for QML applications

It's not too difficult to write a plugin for Qt/C++ applications, whereas it's somewhat more complex to create a plugin for the QML applications. The idea is the same, and here we will use a very basic example to demonstrate this topic. Basically, this application will encode the text input as `Base64` and display it. The `Base64` encoding part is implemented in the C++ plugin.

This time, we're going to create the plugin project first, and then complete the QML part. Creating a plugin project for a QML application shares the same procedure. Navigate to **Libraries | C++ Library**, and then select **Qt Plugin** with the name as `Base64Plugin`. Its project file, `Base64Plugin.pro`, is pasted here:

```
QT          += core qml

TARGET = qmlbase64Plugin
TEMPLATE = lib
CONFIG += plugin

DESTDIR = ../imports/Base64

SOURCES += base64.cpp \
           base64plugin.cpp

HEADERS += base64.h \
           base64plugin.h

OTHER_FILES += \
           qmldir
```

We set DESTDIR to ../imports/Base64 for the sake of convenience. You can change this to some other path, but you may need to make some relevant changes later to be able to import this plugin.

This project consists of two C++ classes. The Base64 class will later be exported to QML, whereas Base64Plugin registers the Base64 class. The former class' base64.h header file is as follows:

```
#ifndef BASE64_H
#define BASE64_H

#include <QObject>

class Base64 : public QObject
{
   Q_OBJECT

   public:
      explicit Base64(QObject *parent = 0);

   public slots:
      QString get(QString);
};

#endif // BASE64_H
```

The base.cpp counterpart defines the get function, as shown in the following code:

```
#include "base64.h"

Base64::Base64(QObject *parent) :
  QObject(parent)
{
}

QString Base64::get(QString in)
{
    return QString::fromLocal8Bit(in.toLocal8Bit().toBase64());
}
```

The tricky part is in the Base64Plugin class, which is not identical to the previous plugin class. Its base64plugin.h header file is shown here:

```
#ifndef BASE64PLUGIN_H
#define BASE64PLUGIN_H

#include <QQmlExtensionPlugin>


class Base64Plugin : public QQmlExtensionPlugin
{
  Q_OBJECT
  Q_PLUGIN_METADATA(IID "org.qt-project.Qt.QmlExtensionInterface")

  public:
    void registerTypes(const char *uri);
};

#endif // BASE64PLUGIN_H
```

With the QQmlExtensionPlugin subclass, we're able to write our own QML plugin. In fact, this class is used to declare the Base64 class for QML. Also note that since IID in Q_PLUGIN_METADATA is fixed, you probably don't want to change it. As a subclass, it has to reimplement the registerTypes function, which simply registers the class(es). The detailed definition is located in the baseplugin.cpp file whose contents are as shown in the following code:

```
#include <QtQml>
#include "base64plugin.h"
#include "base64.h"
```

```
void Base64Plugin::registerTypes(const char *uri)
{
    Q_ASSERT(uri == QLatin1String("Base64"));
    qmlRegisterType<Base64>(uri, 1, 0, "Base64");
}
```

The Q_ASSERT macro will ensure that the plugin is located inside the Base64 directory. If not, it'll print a warning message containing the source code, filename, and line number. Note that uri, which is expected to be Base64 in this case, is the module name for QML. Below this line, qmlRegisterType is a template function where you need to put the class name, Base64, inside brackets. These arguments will register the class with Base64 as the QML name with Version 1.0.

A last piece is needed to declare a loadable plugin, which is the qmldir file. Note that it has no extension name. This file defines the module name and relevant files in the directory. Here is the content:

```
module Base64
plugin qmlbase64Plugin
```

We need to put this file in the ../imports/Base64 directory, which is the DESTDIR of Base64Plugin. Along with a few lines in the QML application project's main.cpp file, QML can then import a plugin as it imports any other Qt Quick modules.

It's time to create a new Qt Quick application project now. The project name is simply QML_Plugin and we move the Base64Plugin class into the QML_Plugin directory, which enables the Qt Creator syntax to highlight the Base64Plugin class. Here is the content of main.qml:

```
import QtQuick 2.3
import QtQuick.Controls 1.2
import Base64 1.0

ApplicationWindow {
    visible: true
    width: 180
    height: 100
    title: qsTr("QML Plugin")

    Base64 {
        id: b64
    }

    Column {
        spacing: 6
```

```
            anchors {left: parent.left; right: parent.right; top:
              parent.top; bottom: parent.bottom; leftMargin: 6;
                rightMargin: 6; topMargin: 6; bottomMargin: 6}
            Label {
              text: "Input"
            }
            TextField {
              id: input
              width: parent.width
              placeholderText: "Input string here"
              onEditingFinished: bt.text = b64.get(text)
            }
            Label {
              text: "Base64 Encoded"
            }
            TextField {
              id: bt
              readOnly: true
              width: parent.width
            }
          }
        }
      }
```

Remember to state import Base64 1.0 at the very beginning of the code so that our plugin can be loaded. Then, Base64 is just like other QML types we have used before. In the onEditingFinished handler of input TextField, we use the get function, which is in the Base64 class, to set bt.text to the corresponding Base64 class-encoded string.

You may wonder how a QML string type is converted to a QString object. Well, it's implicitly converted between QML and Qt/C++. There are plenty of these conversions for commonly-seen QML data types and Qt data classes. For details, you can look at the Qt documentation to see the full list.

Another thing is that we need to change main.cpp, as mentioned before. Similar to the Qt/C++ case, we use the QDir class to get an application directory and change it to ../imports. Be aware that you should use addImportPath instead of addPluginPath to add ../imports to the QML engine's module search path. This is because we use Base64 as a module, which should be located in the imports path. Meanwhile, the plugin path is for native plugins of imported modules, which are stated in qmldir. The content of the main.cpp file is as follows:

```cpp
#include <QApplication>
#include <QDir>
#include <QQmlApplicationEngine>

int main(int argc, char *argv[])
{
  QApplication app(argc, argv);

  QQmlApplicationEngine engine;
  QDir pluginDir = app.applicationDirPath();
  pluginDir.cdUp();
  pluginDir.cdUp();
  pluginDir.cd("imports");
  engine.addImportPath(pluginDir.absolutePath());
  engine.load(QUrl(QStringLiteral("qrc:/main.qml")));

  return app.exec();
}
```

In order to run this application, perform the following steps:

1. Build `Base64Plugin`.

2. Copy the `qmldir` file into the `../imports/Base64` directory (the `imports` folder should be located in the same place as `plugins`).

3. Build and run the `QML_Plugin` project.

You can test this application by inputting any string in the first input field and just pressing *Enter*. One scenario for this application is to encode your e-mail address to avoid a web spider, as shown here:

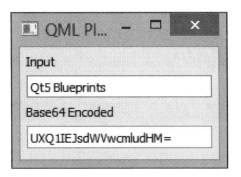

If the module isn't well located, the application won't show up and it'll complain that `Base64` is not installed. If that happens, make sure you add the correct path in `main.cpp` and there is a `qmldir` file inside the `Base64` folder.

Summary

It is somewhat difficult to get started on writing plugins. However, after some basic practice, you'll find that it's actually easier than it looks. For Qt Widgets applications, plugins simply extend the application in a flexible way. Meanwhile, they enable developers to devise new forms for QML applications. We also covered using the `subdirs` project to manage multiple subprojects. Even if you don't plan to write plugins, this chapter covered painting-related stuff that is crucial for GUI application development, including `QPainter`, `paintEvent`, and `resizeEvent`.

In the next chapter, we're going to talk about network programming and multithreading in Qt.

6
Getting Wired and Managing Downloads

Network modules have become crucial nowadays and are also a must-have feature for development frameworks; therefore, Qt does provide APIs for network programming. Sit tight, we're going to get wired and download files from the network. In addition to this, threading is included in this chapter, which is a vital programming skill to avoid blocking. This chapter's topics are listed as follows:

- Introducing Qt network programming
- Utilizing QNetworkAccessManager
- Making use of the progress bar
- Writing multithreaded applications
- Managing a system network session

Introducing Qt network programming

Qt supports network programming and provides lots of high-level APIs to ease your work. QNetworkRequest, QNetworkReply, and QNetworkAccessManager use common protocols to perform network operations. Qt also offers lower-level classes to represent low level network concepts.

In this chapter, we're going to utilize the high-level APIs that Qt has offered to write a downloader to retrieve the Internet files and save them to your disk. As I mentioned earlier, the application will need the QNetworkRequest, QNetworkReply, and QNetworkAccessManager classes.

Firstly, all network requests are represented by the QNetworkRequest class, which is a general container for information associated with a request, including the header and encryption. Currently, HTTP, FTP, and local file URLs are supported for uploading and downloading.

Once a request has been created, the QNetworkAccessManager class is used to dispatch it and emits signals, reporting the progress. Then, it creates the reply to a network request, represented by the QNetworkReply class. At the same time, the signals provided by QNetworkReply can be used to monitor each reply individually. Some developers will discard the reference to the reply and use the QNetworkAccessManager class's signals for that purpose, though. All replies can be handled synchronously or asynchronously, because QNetworkReply is a subclass of QIODevice, which means that it's possible to implement nonblocking operations.

Here is a diagram that describes the relationship between these classes:

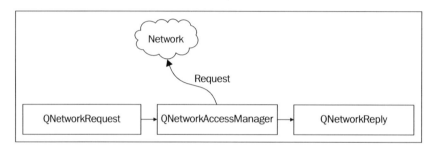

Likewise, the network-related stuff is offered in the network module. To use this module, you need to edit the project file and add network to QT. Now, create a new Qt Widget Application project and edit the project file. In our Downloader_Demo example, the downloader_demo.pro project file is shown here:

```
QT          += core gui network

greaterThan(QT_MAJOR_VERSION, 4): QT += widgets

TARGET = Downloader_Demo
TEMPLATE = app


SOURCES +=  main.cpp\
            mainwindow.cpp \
            downloader.cpp \
            downloaddialog.cpp
```

```
HEADERS   += mainwindow.h \
             downloader.h \
             downloaddialog.h

FORMS     += mainwindow.ui \
             downloaddialog.ui
```

Utilizing QNetworkAccessManager

Now, we're going to discover how to write an application that is able to download files from other locations. By other locations, we mean that you can download files from a local position; it doesn't have to be an Internet address, since the local file URLs are supported by Qt as well.

First of all, let's create a `Downloader` class that will use `QNetworkAccessManager` to do the downloading work for us. The `downloader.h` header file is pasted shown as follows:

```
#ifndef DOWNLOADER_H
#define DOWNLOADER_H

#include <QObject>
#include <QNetworkAccessManager>
#include <QNetworkRequest>
#include <QNetworkReply>

class Downloader : public QObject
{
  Q_OBJECT
public:
  explicit Downloader(QObject *parent = 0);

public slots:
  void download(const QUrl &url, const QString &file);

signals:
  void errorString(const QString &);
  void available(bool);
  void running(bool);
  void downloadProgress(qint64, qint64);
```

```
private:
  QNetworkAccessManager *naManager;
  QString saveFile;

  void saveToDisk(QNetworkReply *);

private slots:
  void onDownloadFinished(QNetworkReply *);
};


#endif // DOWNLOADER_H
```

We expose the download slot to get the URL and the saving target. Accordingly, saveFile is used to store the saving target. In addition to this, we use an naManager object of the QNetworkAccessManager class to manage the downloading process.

Let's check the definitions of these functions in the downloader.cpp file. In the following constructor, we connect the naManager object's finished signal to the onDownloadFinished slot. Therefore, when a network connection is finished, a relevant QNetworkReply reference will be passed via this signal.

```
Downloader::Downloader(QObject *parent)  :
  QObject(parent)
{
  naManager = new QNetworkAccessManager(this);
  connect(naManager, &QNetworkAccessManager::finished, this,
    &Downloader::onDownloadFinished);
}
```

Accordingly, in the onDownloadFinished slot, we have to handle QNetworkReply with caution. If there is any error, which means that the download has failed, we expose the errorString() function by the errorString signal. Otherwise, we call the saveToDisk function to save the file to the disk. Then, we use deleteLater() to release the QNetworkReply object safely. As stated in the Qt documentation, it's not safe to use the delete statement directly; since it's finished, we emit the available and running signals. Those signals will later be used to change the user interface.

```
void Downloader::onDownloadFinished(QNetworkReply *reply)
{
  if (reply->error() != QNetworkReply::NoError) {
    emit errorString(reply->errorString());
  }
```

```
   else {
     saveToDisk(reply);
   }
   reply->deleteLater();
   emit available(true);
   emit running(false);
 }
```

In the `saveToDisk` function, we just implement `QFile` to save all the downloaded data to the disk. This is feasible because `QNetworkReply` inherits from `QIODevice`. Therefore, in addition to the networking APIs, you can treat `QNetworkReply` as a normal `QIODevice` object. In this case, use the `readAll()` function to get all data:

```
 void Downloader::saveToDisk(QNetworkReply *reply)
 {
   QFile f(saveFile);
   f.open(QIODevice::WriteOnly | QIODevice::Truncate);
   f.write(reply->readAll());
   f.close();
 }
```

Finally, let's see inside the `download` function that will be used by `MainWindow` later. Firstly, we store the saved file to `saveFile`. Then, we construct `QNetworkRequest` `req` using the `QUrl` object, `url`. Next, we send `req` to the `naManager` object of `QNetworkAccessManager`, while saving the reference to the created `QNetworkManager` object to `reply`. After this, we connect the two `downloadProgress` signals together, which is simply exposing the `downloadProgress` signal of the reply. At last, we end up emitting two signals, indicating the availability and running status respectively.

```
 void Downloader::download(const QUrl &url, const QString &file)
 {
   saveFile = file;
   QNetworkRequest req(url);
   QNetworkReply *reply = naManager->get(req);
   connect(reply, &QNetworkReply::downloadProgress, this,
     &Downloader::downloadProgress);
   emit available(false);
   emit running(true);
 }
```

We described the `Downloader` class. Now, we're going to add `DownloadDialog` by navigating to **Qt Designer | Dialog with Buttons Bottom**. This class is used to get the URL and save the path for the user. For the design of `downloaddialog.ui`, we use the two `QLineEdit` objects to get the URL and saved path respectively. One of the object names is `urlEdit`, and the other is `saveAsEdit`. In order to open a file dialog for the user to choose the saving location, a `saveAsButton` attribute of `QPushButton` is added to the right-hand side of `saveAsEdit`. The following screenshot shows you the layout of this UI file:

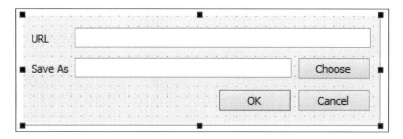

You need to change the layout of this dialog to **Lay Out in a Grid**. In a similar way as we did before, in order to pass the values to the main window, we need to delete the default `accepted` signal and slot connection in **Signals & Slots Editor**.

The contents of this class's `downloaddialog.h` header file are shown here:

```
#ifndef DOWNLOADDIALOG_H
#define DOWNLOADDIALOG_H

#include <QDialog>

namespace Ui {
  class DownloadDialog;
}

class DownloadDialog : public QDialog
{
  Q_OBJECT

public:
  explicit DownloadDialog(QWidget *parent = 0);
  ~DownloadDialog();

signals:
  void accepted(const QUrl &, const QString &);
```

```
private:
  Ui::DownloadDialog *ui;

private slots:
  void onButtonAccepted();
  void onSaveAsButtonClicked();
};


#endif // DOWNLOADDIALOG_H
```

As you can see, a new signal named accepted is added to pass the URL and save the location. Besides, the two private slots are used to handle the accepted event of the button box and the saveAsButtonClicked signal, respectively.

The definitions are in the downloaddialog.cpp source file, which is shown here:

```
#include <QFileDialog>
#include "downloaddialog.h"
#include "ui_downloaddialog.h"

DownloadDialog::DownloadDialog(QWidget *parent) :
  QDialog(parent),
  ui(new Ui::DownloadDialog)
{
  ui->setupUi(this);

  connect(ui->buttonBox, &QDialogButtonBox::accepted, this,
    &DownloadDialog::onButtonAccepted);
  connect(ui->saveAsButton, &QPushButton::clicked, this,
    &DownloadDialog::onSaveAsButtonClicked);
}

DownloadDialog::~DownloadDialog()
{
  delete ui;
}

void DownloadDialog::onButtonAccepted()
{
  emit accepted(QUrl(ui->urlEdit->text()),
    ui->saveAsEdit->text());
  this->accept();
}


void DownloadDialog::onSaveAsButtonClicked()
```

```
  {
    QString str = QFileDialog::getSaveFileName(this, "Save As");
    if (!str.isEmpty()) {
      ui->saveAsEdit->setText(str);
    }
  }
}
```

In the constructor of `DownloadDialog`, just connect the signals and slots. In the `onButtonAccepted` slot, we emit the `accepted` signal, which is to pass the URL and the saving path, where a temporary `QUrl` class is constructed using the text of `urlEdit`. Then, the `accept` function is invoked to close the dialog. Meanwhile, in the `onSaveAsButtonClicked` slot function, we use the `static` function provided by the `QFileDialog` class to obtain the saving location. Do nothing if the `QString` return is empty; this means that the user may have clicked on **Cancel** in the file dialog.

Making use of the progress bar

An intuitive way to indicate the downloading progress is by using a progress bar. In Qt, it is the `QProgressBar` class that provides a horizontal or vertical progress bar widget. It uses `minimum`, `value`, and `maximum` to determine the completed percentage. The percentage is calculated by the formula, `(value – minimum) / (maximum – minimum)`. We'll use this useful widget in our example application by performing the following steps:

1. Go back to the `MainWindow` class.
2. Edit the `mainwindow.ui` file in the **Design** mode.
3. Drag **Push Button** and rename it as `newDownloadButton` with `New Download` as its text.
4. Drag **Progress Bar** just beneath `newDownloadButton`.
5. Change the layout to **Lay Out Vertically**.
6. Uncheck `textVisible` in the `progressBar` widget's property.

The push button, `newDownloadButton`, is used to popup `DownloadDialog` to get a new download task. We need to apply some modifications to `mainwindow.h`, as suggested here:

```
#ifndef MAINWINDOW_H
#define MAINWINDOW_H

#include <QMainWindow>
#include "downloader.h"
```

```
#include "downloaddialog.h"

namespace Ui {
  class MainWindow;
}

class MainWindow : public QMainWindow
{
  Q_OBJECT

public:
  explicit MainWindow(QWidget *parent = 0);
  ~MainWindow();

private:
  Ui::MainWindow *ui;
  Downloader *downloader;
  DownloadDialog *ddlg;

private slots:
  void onNewDownloadButtonPressed();
  void showMessage(const QString &);
  void onDownloadProgress(qint64, qint64);
};

#endif // MAINWINDOW_H
```

In order to use the `Downloader` and `DownloadDialog` classes, we have to include them in the `header` file. Then, we can include them as the `private` pointers. For the `private` slots, `onNewDownloadButtonPressed` is used to handle the `newDownloadButton` clicked signal. While `showMessage` is a slot function that displays the message on status bar, the last one, `onDownloadProgress`, is used to update the progress bar.

Similarly, for the `mainwindow.cpp` source file, we connect the signals and slots in the constructor, shown as follows:

```
MainWindow::MainWindow(QWidget *parent) :
  QMainWindow(parent),
  ui(new Ui::MainWindow)
{
  ui->setupUi(this);
  ui->progressBar->setVisible(false);
```

```
    downloader = new Downloader(this);

    connect(ui->newDownloadButton, &QPushButton::clicked, this,
      &MainWindow::onNewDownloadButtonPressed);
    connect(downloader, &Downloader::errorString, this,
      &MainWindow::showMessage);
    connect(downloader, &Downloader::downloadProgress, this,
      &MainWindow::onDownloadProgress);
    connect(downloader, &Downloader::available,
      ui->newDownloadButton, &QPushButton::setEnabled);
    connect(downloader, &Downloader::running, ui->progressBar,
      &QProgressBar::setVisible);
}
```

Before beginning to create these connections, we need to hide the progress bar and create a new `Downloader` class, using `MainWindow` as the `QObject` parent. Meanwhile, in these connections, the first one is to connect the `newDownloadButton` clicked signal. Then, we connect the `errorString` signal of downloader to `showMessage`, which enables the status bar to show the error message directly. Next, we connect the `downloadProgress` signal to our `onDownloadProgress` handler. As for the available and running signals, they're connected to control the availability and visibility of `newDownloadButton` and `progressBar`, respectively.

Inside the `onNewDownloadButtonPressed` slot function, we construct a `DownloadDialog` object, `ddlg`, then connect the accepted signal of `DownloadDialog` to the `Downloader` class's download slot. Then, use `exec` to run the dialog and block the event loop. After this, we call `deleteLater` to safely release the resource allocated for `ddlg`.

```
void MainWindow::onNewDownloadButtonPressed()
{
  ddlg = new DownloadDialog(this);
  connect(ddlg, &DownloadDialog::accepted, downloader,
    &Downloader::download);
  ddlg->exec();
  ddlg->deleteLater();
}
```

As for the `showMessage` slot function, it simply calls the `showMessage` function of `statusBar` with a three second timeout, as shown here:

```
void MainWindow::showMessage(const QString &es)
{
  ui->statusBar->showMessage(es, 3000);
}
```

At last, we can update the progress bar via the `onDownloadProgress` function, which is shown in the following code. Since the `minimum` value is `0` by default, we don't need to change it. Instead, we change the `maximum` value to the total bytes of the download, and `value` to the current downloaded bytes. Note that if the total size is unknown, then the value of the total size is `-1`, which will happen to make the progress bar display in a busy style.

```
void MainWindow::onDownloadProgress(qint64 r, qint64 t)
{
    ui->progressBar->setMaximum(t);
    ui->progressBar->setValue(r);
}
```

Now, give the application a run and click on the **New Download** button. The **Add New Download** dialog will pop up, where you can add a new download task as shown here:

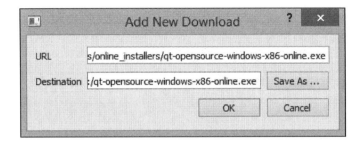

Click on **OK**, if there is no error; a progress bar is expected to show up and display the current download progress, shown as follows:

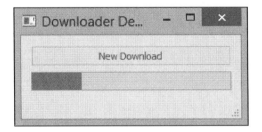

As you can see, the **New Download** button is not enabled now, since it is associated with the available signal of `downloader`. Besides, the progress bar won't even show if `downloader` isn't running.

While this downloader demo still lacks a basic function, which is to cancel downloading, it is, in fact, easy to implement. There is a slot function called `abort` in the `QNetworkReply` class. You may have to store the reference to `QNetworkReply` and then call abort if some button in `MainWindow` is clicked. This won't be demonstrated here. It has been left up to you to practice on your own.

Writing multithreaded applications

I bet multithread or threading isn't unfamiliar to you. Using other threads saves the GUI application from freezing. If the application runs on a single thread, it'll get stuck if there it's a synchronous time-consuming operation. Multiple threads make application running much smoother. Although most of the Qt Network APIs are nonblocking, it is not that difficult to practice on it.

Qt provides a `QThread` class to implement threading on all supported platforms. In other words, we don't need to write platform-specific code utilizing POSIX Threads or a Win32 API. Instead, `QThread` provides a platform-independent way to manage threads. A `QThread` object manages a thread within the program, which begins executing in `run()` and ends when calling `quit()` or `exit()`.

For some historical reason, it's still possible to subclass `QThread` and put the blocking or time-consuming code in the reimplemented `run()` function. However, it's considered an incorrect practice and is not recommended to do so. The right way is to use `QObject::moveToThread`, which will be demonstrated later.

We're going to put the `Downloader::download` function into a new thread. In fact, it's the `QNetworkAccessManager::get` function that will be moved onto another thread. Let's create a new C++ class, `DownloadWorker`, whose `downloadworker.h` header file is pasted as follows:

```
#ifndef DOWNLOADWORKER_H
#define DOWNLOADWORKER_H

#include <QObject>
#include <QNetworkReply>
#include <QNetworkRequest>
#include <QNetworkAccessManager>

class DownloadWorker : public QObject
{
  Q_OBJECT
```

```
public slots:
  void doDownload(const QUrl &url, QNetworkAccessManager *nm);

signals:
  void downloadProgress(qint64, qint64);
};


#endif // DOWNLOADWORKER_H
```

The constructor is removed from the code because we can't make a child object that will be in another thread. This is almost the only limitation of QThread. In contrast to this, you can connect signals and slots between different threads without any problems.

Don't split parent and children between threads. Parent objects and children objects can only be in the same thread.

We declare the doDownload slot function to do the QNetworkAccessManager::get function work for us. On the other hand, the downloadProgress signal is used to expose the downloadProgress signal of QNetworkReply as we did. The contents of downloadworker.cpp is shown as follows:

```
#include "downloadworker.h"

void DownloadWorker::doDownload(const QUrl &url,
  QNetworkAccessManager *nm)
{
  QNetworkRequest req(url);
  QNetworkReply *reply = nm->get(req);
  connect(reply, &QNetworkReply::downloadProgress, this,
    &DownloadWorker::downloadProgress);
}
```

The preceding code is an example of a simple worker class. Now, we have to change the Downloader class to use the DownloadWorker class. The header file of the Downloader class, downloader.h, needs a few modifications, shown here:

```
#ifndef DOWNLOADER_H
#define DOWNLOADER_H

#include <QObject>
#include <QNetworkAccessManager>
#include <QNetworkRequest>
#include <QNetworkReply>
#include <QThread>
```

```
#include "downloadworker.h"

class Downloader : public QObject
{
  Q_OBJECT
public:
  explicit Downloader(QObject *parent = 0);
  ~Downloader();

public slots:
  void download(const QUrl &url, const QString &file);

signals:
  void errorString(const QString &);
  void available(bool);
  void running(bool);
  void downloadProgress(qint64, qint64);

private:
  QString saveFile;
  QNetworkAccessManager *naManager;
  DownloadWorker *worker;
  QThread workerThread;

  void saveToDisk(QNetworkReply *);

private slots:
  void onDownloadFinished(QNetworkReply *);
};

#endif // DOWNLOADER_H
```

As you can see, we have declared a new `private` member, `workerThread`, which is a type of `QThread`. Also, a `DownloadWorker` object worker has been declared as well. There are more changes in the `downloader.cpp` source file, as displayed here:

```
#include <QFile>
#include "downloader.h"

Downloader::Downloader(QObject *parent) :
  QObject(parent)
{
  naManager = new QNetworkAccessManager(this);
  worker = new DownloadWorker;
  worker->moveToThread(&workerThread);
```

```
  connect(naManager, &QNetworkAccessManager::finished, this,
    &Downloader::onDownloadFinished);
  connect(&workerThread, &QThread::finished, worker,
    &DownloadWorker::deleteLater);
  connect(worker, &DownloadWorker::downloadProgress, this,
    &Downloader::downloadProgress);

  workerThread.start();
}


Downloader::~Downloader()
{
  workerThread.quit();
  workerThread.wait();
}

void Downloader::download(const QUrl &url, const QString &file)
{
  saveFile = file;
  worker->doDownload(url, naManager);
  emit available(false);
  emit running(true);
}

void Downloader::onDownloadFinished(QNetworkReply *reply)
{
  if (reply->error() != QNetworkReply::NoError) {
    emit errorString(reply->errorString());
  }
  else {
    saveToDisk(reply);
  }
  reply->deleteLater();
  emit available(true);
  emit running(false);
}

void Downloader::saveToDisk(QNetworkReply *reply)
{
  QFile f(saveFile);
  f.open(QIODevice::WriteOnly | QIODevice::Truncate);
  f.write(reply->readAll());
  f.close();
}
```

In the constructor, we will create a new `DownloadWorker` class, and move it to another thread, `workerThread`. By connecting the `finished` signal of `workerThread` to the `deleteLater` function of `worker`, the resources of `worker` can be deleted safely after the exit of `workerThread`. Then, we need to expose `downloadProgress` again, since it's moved into `worker`. At last, we call the `start()` function, to start `workerThread`.

As a reverse operation, we call the `quit()` function to exit `workerThread` and then use `wait()` to ensure it quits successfully.

Since a lot of code has been moved into the `doDownload` function of `worker`, we only need to call `doDownload` of `worker` here. In fact, the function calling is inter-thread, which means that the main thread won't be blocked by that statement.

Since `get` is not blocking, you may not feel the difference. However, I'm sure you have some applications that have frozen, which therefore need to be modified to adapt to `QThread`. Always remember to put only the background blocking operations in another thread. This is mainly because these operations are easily separated from GUI into single objects without parents or children. Due to this limitation, almost all the GUI objects must be in the same thread, which is the main thread in most cases.

Managing a system network session

In addition to networking applications, Qt also provides you with cross-platform APIs to control network interfaces and access points. Although it's not very common to control the network state, there are some certain situations where it's required to do this.

First, I'd like to introduce `QNetworkConfigurationManager` to you. This class manages the network configurations provided by the system. It enables you access to them, as well as to detect the system's capabilities during runtime. The network configuration is presented by the `QNetworkConfiguration` class, which abstracts a set of configuration options concerning how a network interface has to be configured in order to connect to the target network. To control the network session, you need to use the `QNetworkSession` class. This class provides you with control over the system's access points and enables session management. It also enables you to control network interfaces that are represented by the `QNetworkInterface` class. To help you figure out this relationship, a diagram is shown here:

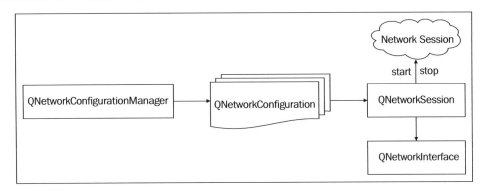

As you can see, the structure is similar to QNetworkAccessManager, QNetworkReply, and QNetworkRequest. Especially, there is another manager class. Let's see how to deal with these classes in practice.

Create a new Qt Widgets Application project as usual. The example regarding this topic is called NetworkManager_Demo. Remember to add network to Qt in your project file, as we did in the previous example. Then, edit mainwindow.ui in the **Design** mode and perform the following steps:

1. Remove the status bar, menu bar, and tool bar since we don't need them in this application.

2. Add **List View** (under the **Item Views (Model-Based)** category).

3. Drag **Vertical Layout** to the right of listView.

4. Change **Lay out** in **MainWindow** to **Lay Out Horizontally**.

5. Drag **Label** into verticalLayout and rename it as onlineStatus.

6. Drag **Progress Bar** into verticalLayout. Change its maximum value to 0 and uncheck textVisible so that it can be used as a busy indicator.

7. Add three **Push Button** buttons; **Refresh**, **Connect**, and **Disconnect**; beneath the progress bar. Their object names are refreshButton, connectButton, and disconnectButton, respectively.

8. At last, drag **Vertical Spacer** between progressBar and onlineStatus to separate them.

As usual, we need to do some declarations in `mainwindow.h` header file as shown here:

```
#ifndef MAINWINDOW_H
#define MAINWINDOW_H

#include <QMainWindow>
#include <QNetworkConfigurationManager>
#include <QNetworkConfiguration>
#include <QNetworkSession>
#include <QStandardItemModel>

namespace Ui {
  class MainWindow;
}

class MainWindow : public QMainWindow
{
  Q_OBJECT

public:
  explicit MainWindow(QWidget *parent = 0);
  ~MainWindow();

private:
  Ui::MainWindow *ui;
  QNetworkConfigurationManager *networkConfManager;
  QStandardItemModel *confListModel;

private slots:
  void onOnlineStateChanged(bool isOnline);
  void onConfigurationChanged(const QNetworkConfiguration
    &config);
  void onRefreshClicked();
  void onRefreshCompleted();
  void onConnectClicked();
  void onDisconnectClicked();
};

#endif // MAINWINDOW_H
```

In this case, we only utilize the `QNetworkConfigurationManager`, `QNetworkConfiguration`, and `QNetworkSession` classes to manage the system network sessions. Therefore, we need to include them in an appropriate location.

Note that we only need to declare a `private` member, in this case `networkConfManager`, of the `QNetworkConfigurationManager` class, because the `QNetworkConfiguration` can be retrieved from this manager, while `QNetworkSession` is bound to `QNetworkConfiguration`.

As for `QStandardItemModel`, remember the model/view stuff in *Chapter 3, Cooking an RSS Reader with Qt Quick*. The only difference between that chapter and this one is that we wrote QML in the former. However, we are using a C++ application in this chapter. They share the same concept, though, and it's just the tool that changes. `QStandardItemModel *confListModel` is the exact model of `listView` in the UI file.

Last, but not least, is the declaration of some slots. Apart from the button click handlers, the first two are used to monitor the network system. This is explained later.

Let's edit the `mainwindow.cpp` file and take a look at the constructor of `MainWindow`:

```
MainWindow::MainWindow(QWidget *parent)  :
  QMainWindow(parent),
  ui(new Ui::MainWindow)
{
  ui->setupUi(this);

  networkConfManager = new QNetworkConfigurationManager(this);
  confListModel = new QStandardItemModel(0, 1, this);

  ui->listView->setModel(confListModel);
  ui->progressBar->setVisible(false);

  connect(networkConfManager,
    &QNetworkConfigurationManager::onlineStateChanged, this,
      &MainWindow::onOnlineStateChanged);
  connect(networkConfManager,
    &QNetworkConfigurationManager::configurationChanged, this,
      &MainWindow::onConfigurationChanged);
  connect(networkConfManager,
    &QNetworkConfigurationManager::updateCompleted, this,
      &MainWindow::onRefreshCompleted);

  connect(ui->refreshButton, &QPushButton::clicked, this,
    &MainWindow::onRefreshClicked);
  connect(ui->connectButton, &QPushButton::clicked, this,
    &MainWindow::onConnectClicked);
  connect(ui->disconnectButton, &QPushButton::clicked, this,
    &MainWindow::onDisconnectClicked);

  onOnlineStateChanged(networkConfManager->isOnline());
  onRefreshClicked();
}
```

We construct QNetworkConfigurationManager with this object, also known as MainWindow as its QObject parent. Then, we look at the construction of confListModel. The arguments are the count of row, the count of column, and the QObject parent, which is this as usual. We will use only one column because we use **List View** to display the data. If you use **Table View**, you will probably use more columns. Then, we bind this model to listView of ui. After this, we hide progressBar because it's a busy indicator, which only shows up when there is work running. There will be several connect statements before we call two member functions explicitly. Among them, you may want to look into the signals of QNetworkConfigurationManager. The onlineStateChanged signal is emitted if the online status of the system is changed, that is, offline from online. The configurationChanged signal is emitted whenever the state of QNetworkConfiguration is changed. Once QNetworkConfigurationManager finished updateConfigurations, the updateCompleted signal will be emitted. In the end of the constructor, we call onOnlineStateChanged directly in order to set up the text of onlineStatus. Similarly, calling onRefreshClicked enables an application to scan for all the network configurations at the start.

As mentioned before, the onOnlineStateChanged function is used to set up onlineStatus. It'll display Online if the system is considered to be connected to another device via an active network interface; otherwise, it'll display Offline. This function's definition is shown as follows:

```
void MainWindow::onOnlineStateChanged(bool isOnline)
{
  ui->onlineStatus->setText(isOnline ? "Online" : "Offline");
}
```

Inside the onConfigurationChanged slot function, which is shown in the following code, we change the item's background color to indicate whether a configuration is active or not. We use the findItems function to get itemList, which contains only some QStandardItem that matches config.name() exactly. However, the configuration name may not be unique. This is why we use a foreach loop to compare the identifier of config, which is a unique string, where the data function is used to retrieve the specific data whose type is QVariant. Then, we use toString to cast it back to QString. QStandardItem enables us set multiple data into one item.

```
void MainWindow::onConfigurationChanged(const
  QNetworkConfiguration &config)
{
  QList<QStandardItem *> itemList =
    confListModel->findItems(config.name());
  foreach (QStandardItem *i, itemList) {
    if (i->data(Qt::UserRole).toString().compare(config.
      identifier()) == 0) {
```

```
    if (config.state().testFlag(QNetworkConfiguration::Active))
      {
      i->setBackground(QBrush(Qt::green));
      }
    else {
      i->setBackground(QBrush(Qt::NoBrush));
      }
    }
  }
}
```

This means that we store `identifier` as a `Qt::UserRole` data. It won't be displayed on the screen; instead, it serves as a specific data carrier, which turns out to be very helpful in this case. Thus, after this, if it's active, we set the background color to green; otherwise, use no brush, which means a default background. Note that the `state` function of `QNetworkConfiguration` returns `StateFlags`, which is actually a `QFlag` template class, where the best practice is to check whether or not a flag is set is to use the `testFlag` function.

Let's check the `onRefreshClicked` function, which is shown in the following code before `onRefreshCompleted`. It'll call `updateConfigurations` of the `QNetworkConfigurationManager *networkConfManager`. This function is a time consuming one, especially if it needs to scan WLAN. Therefore, we show `progressBar` to tell users to be patient and disable `refreshButton`, since it's refreshing.

```
void MainWindow::onRefreshClicked()
{
  ui->progressBar->setVisible(true);
  ui->refreshButton->setEnabled(false);
  networkConfManager->updateConfigurations();
}
```

When the update has been completed, the `updateCompleted` signal is emitted and the `onRefreshCompleted` bound slot is executed. Check the following function shown here, where we need to purge the list. However, instead of calling the `clear` function, we use `removeRows`, which would spare the column. If you're calling `clear`, beware to add the column back; otherwise, there is literally no column, which means that there is no place to put the item. In the `foreach` loop, we add all the configurations that `networkConfManager` has found to `confListModel`. As I mentioned previously, we use the name as displaying `text`, while we set its identifier as a hidden user role data. After the loop, hide `progressBar` as the refreshing is finished, and then enable `refreshButton`.

```
void MainWindow::onRefreshCompleted()
{
  confListModel->removeRows(0, confListModel->rowCount());
  foreach(QNetworkConfiguration c,
    networkConfManager->allConfigurations()) {
    QStandardItem *item = new QStandardItem(c.name());
    item->setData(QVariant(c.identifier()), Qt::UserRole);
    if (c.state().testFlag(QNetworkConfiguration::Active)) {
      item->setBackground(QBrush(Qt::green));
    }
    confListModel->appendRow(item);
  }
  ui->progressBar->setVisible(false);
  ui->refreshButton->setEnabled(true);
}
```

The remaining two are handlers to the connect and disconnect buttons. For connectButton, we show progressBar because it may take a long time to get the IP address from the router. Then, we get identifier from the data of confListModel directly and save it as QString ident, where the currentIndex function of listView will return the current QModelIndex of the view. By using this index, we can get the currently selected data from the model. Then, we construct QNetworkConfiguration from ident by calling configurationFromIdentifier of networkConfManager. The QNetworkSession session is constructed using QNetworkConfiguration. At last, open this network session and wait for 1,000 milliseconds. Then, call deleteLater to safely release the session. Also, hide progressBar after all these works in the end.

```
void MainWindow::onConnectClicked()
{
  ui->progressBar->setVisible(true);
  QString ident =
    confListModel->data(ui->listView->currentIndex(),
      Qt::UserRole).toString();
  QNetworkConfiguration conf =
    networkConfManager->configurationFromIdentifier(ident);
  QNetworkSession *session = new QNetworkSession(conf, this);
  session->open();
  session->waitForOpened(1000);
  session->deleteLater();
  ui->progressBar->setVisible(false);
}
```

```
void MainWindow::onDisconnectClicked()
{
  QString ident =
    confListModel->data(ui->listView->currentIndex(),
      Qt::UserRole).toString();
  QNetworkConfiguration conf =
    networkConfManager->configurationFromIdentifier(ident);
  QNetworkSession *session = new QNetworkSession(conf, this);
  if (networkConfManager->capabilities().testFlag
    (QNetworkConfigurationManager::SystemSessionSupport)) {
    session->close();
  }
  else {
    session->stop();
  }
  session->deleteLater();
}
```

As for `disconnectButton`, the `onDisconnectClicked` handler will do the reverse, which is to stop the network session. The first three lines are identical to those in `onConnectClicked`. However, we then need to test whether the platform supports out-of-process sessions. As stated in the Qt documentation, the result of calling `close` will be as follows:

> *void QNetworkSession::close() [slot]*
>
> *Decreases the session counter on the associated network configuration. If the session counter reaches zero the active network interface is shut down. This also means that state() will only change from Connected to Disconnected if the current session was the last open session.*

However, if the platform doesn't support out-of-process sessions, the `close` function won't stop the interface, in which case we need to use stop instead.

Therefore, we call the `capabilities` function of `networkConfManager` to check whether it has `SystemSessionSupport`. Call `close` if it does, otherwise call `stop`. Then, we just call `deleteLater` to safely release the session.

Now, run this application, and you'll expect it works as the following screenshot:

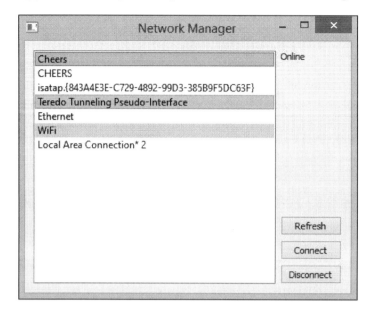

On Windows, the network architecture is different from that of the world of Unix. So, you may find some odd configurations in the list, such as **Teredo Tunneling Pseudo-Interface** in the screenshot. Don't worry about these configurations and just ignore them! Also, there is no Qt API to allow you to connect to a newly discovered encrypted Wi-Fi access point. This is because there is no implementation in place to access the WLAN system passwords. In other words, it can only be used to control the network sessions that are already known to the system.

Summary

In this chapter, you have had a chance to practice what you have learned in the previous chapters while picking up new skills in Qt. So far, you'll have gained an insight into the architecture of Qt that is commonly seen and shared by its submodules. After all, networking and threading will definitely bring your applications to a higher level.

In the next chapter, besides parsing XML and JSON documents, we're going to rock Android with Qt!

7
Parsing JSON and XML Documents to Use Online APIs

In this chapter, you'll find the powerful application, Qt, running on the popular Android devices. Following the introduction of Qt application development for Android, it also utilizes online APIs, which usually return JSON or XML documents. The topics that are covered in this chapter are as follows:

- Setting up Qt for Android
- Parsing JSON results
- Parsing XML results
- Building Qt applications for Android
- Parsing JSON in QML

Setting up Qt for Android

Qt for Android requires at least an API level 10 (for Android 2.3.3 platforms). Most Qt modules are supported, which means your Qt application can be deployed on Android with little or no modification. For development, both Qt Widget-based applications and Qt Quick applications in Qt Creator are supported on Android. However, setting up Qt for Android on a Windows PC is not very straightforward. Therefore, before we venture deeper into anything, let's set up the development environment for Qt on Android.

First, you need to install Qt for Android. If you're using an online installer, remember to select the Android components, as shown in the following screenshot:

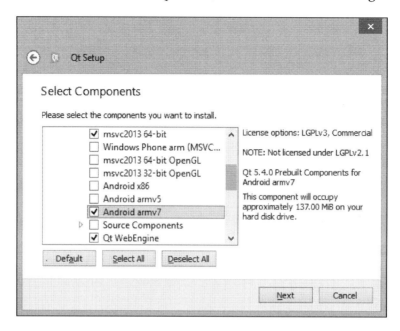

Here, we only chose **Android armv7**, which enables us to deploy applications for ARMv7 Android devices. If you're using an offline installer, download Qt for the Android installer.

Now, let's install a **Java Development Kit** (**JDK**). There is no way to get rid of Java, since Android heavily depends on it. Also, note that you need to install at least Version 6 of JDK, according to http://doc.qt.io/qt-5/androidgs.html. You can download JDK from http://www.oracle.com/technetwork/java/javase/downloads/index.html. You also need to set a JAVA_HOME environment variable in the JDK installation directory, D:\Program Files\Java\jdk1.8.0_25.

Now, let's install two kits from Google, the Android SDK and Android NDK. Always remember to download the latest version; here we use Android SDK r24.0.2 and Android NDK r10b.

After you install the Android SDK, run the SDK Manager. Install or update **Android SDK Tools**, **Android SDK Platform-tools**, **Android SDK Build-tools**, **Google USB Driver**, at least one API level's **SDK Platform**, and **ARM EABI v7a System Image** for the purpose of our task. For this chapter, we installed API 19's **SDK Platform** and **ARM EABI v7a System Image**. Then, edit the PATH environment variable. Add the path of the platform and SDK tools to it with a semicolon as a separator. If D:\ Program Files (x86)\Android\android-sdk is the path of **Android SDK Tools**, it would be as follows:

```
D:\Program Files (x86)\Android\android-sdk\platform-tools;D:\Program
Files (x86)\Android\android-sdk\tools
```

 Android SDK and NDK can be obtained on the Android developer website, http://developer.android.com.

Once you download the NDK, extract the zip file to your hard drive, D:\android-ndk. Then, add an environment variable named ANDROID_NDK_ROOT with the value, D:\android-ndk.

Similar procedures should be applied for Apache Ant. You can download it from http://ant.apache.org/bindownload.cgi. We use Apache Ant 1.9.4 in this book. There is no environment variable that needs to be set here. Now, reboot your computer if you're using Windows so that the environment variables can be refreshed and loaded correctly.

Open AVD Manager and create a new virtual device. You'd better choose a smaller virtual device such as Nexus S for this exercise, as shown in the following screenshot. Feel free to change it if you want, but remember to tick **Use Host GPU**, which will make the virtual device use GLES to accelerate the graphics. If you haven't turned that on, you'll get an extremely slow virtual device that might even be too sluggish to test applications on.

Now, open Qt Creator; navigate to **Tools | Options**. See if Qt Version in **Build & Run** has an Android entry. You have to manually add Qt for Android if it's not there. Then, switch to the **Android** options, set up JDK, Android SDK, Android NDK, and Ant, as shown in the following screenshot:

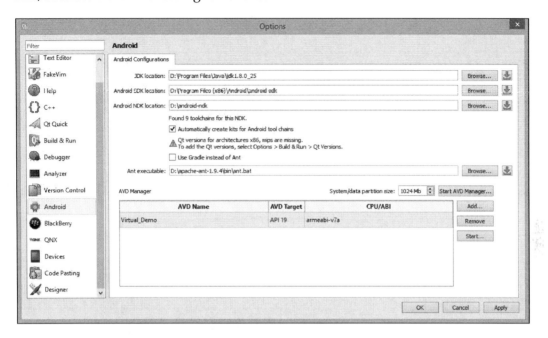

The warning for missing architectures can be safely ignored because we won't develop applications for MIPS and x86 Android in this chapter. However, pay attention to it if you need to deploy your applications on these hardware platforms.

Click on **Apply** and switch to the **Devices** options. There should be a **Run on Android** item in the **Device** combobox. An auto-detected **Android for armeabi-v7a** is expected if you navigate to **Build & Run | Kits** now.

Now, let's test if we can run a Qt application on our virtual Android device. Open AVD Manager and start the virtual device. We start it first because it could take a lot of time. Then, open Qt Creator and make a simple application.

1. Create a new Qt Widget-based application project.

2. Select **Android for armeabi-v7a Kit**.

3. Edit `mainwindow.ui` and drag a label to `centralWidget`.

4. Change the **MainWindow** page's layout to **Lay Out Vertically** (or others) so that the widgets will be stretched automatically.

5. Change the label's text to `Hello Android!` or something else.

Wait for the time-consuming virtual Android device until it's fully started. If it's not, click on **Run** and wait for a few minutes. You'll see this application running on our virtual Android device. As seen in the following screenshot, the Qt for Android development environment is set up successfully. So, we can move on and write an application that can use a camera to take photos:

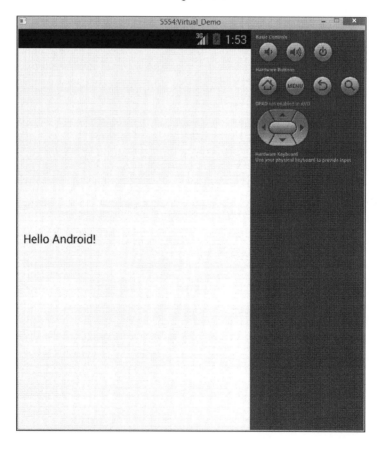

Testing an application on a desktop while it's incomplete, and then testing it on a mobile platform would save plenty of time compared to testing on the virtual Android device all the time. In addition to this, it's much faster to test on a real device than a virtual one.

Instead of tolerating a slow emulator, we're going to first develop the application on a desktop, then deploy it on an actual Android device and see if there is anything mismatched or inappropriate for mobile devices. Make any relevant changes accordingly. This could save you plenty of time. However, it still takes a longer time, even though the actual Android device is much more responsive than the virtual one.

Parsing JSON results

There are tons of companies that provide developers APIs to access to their services, including the dictionary, weather, and so on. In this chapter, we'll use Yahoo! Weather as an example to show you how to use its online API to get weather data. For more details about Yahoo! Weather API, refer to `https://developer.yahoo.com/weather/`.

Now, let's create a new project named `Weather_Demo`, which is a Qt Widget-based application project. As usual, let's first design the UI.

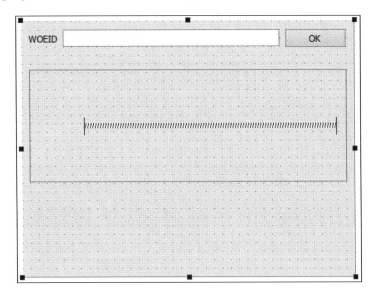

We've removed the menu bar, tool bar, and status bar as we did before. Then, we added a **Label**, **Line Edit**, and **Push Button** on top of `centralWidget`. Their object names are `woeidLabel`, `woeidEdit`, and `okButton`, respectively. After this, another label named `locationLabel` is used to display the location returned from the API. The red rectangle is **Horizontal Layout**, which consists of `tempLabel` and `windLabel`, which are both **Label** and are separated by **Horizontal Spacer**. Append **Label**, whose object name is `attrLabel`, and then change its alignment to `AlignRight` and `AlignBottom`.

Where On Earth ID (WOEID) is a 32-bit identifier that is unique and nonrepetitive. By using WOEID, we can avoid duplicity. However, this also means that we need to find out what WOEID is used for our location. Luckily, there are several websites that provide you with easy-to-use online tools to get the WOEID. One of them is the Zourbuth project, **Yahoo! WOEID Lookup**, which can be accessed at `http://zourbuth.com/tools/woeid/`.

Now, let's move on and focus on the parsing of API results. We created a new C++ class, `Weather`, to deal with the Yahoo! Weather API. I'd like to introduce you to parsing the **JSON (JavaScript Object Notation)** results before XML. However, before we cook the `Weather` class, remember to add network to `QT` in the project file. In this case, the `Weather_Demo.pro` project file looks like this:

```
QT          += core gui network

greaterThan(QT_MAJOR_VERSION, 4): QT += widgets

TARGET = Weather_Demo
TEMPLATE = app

SOURCES += main.cpp\
        mainwindow.cpp \
        weather.cpp

HEADERS  += mainwindow.h \
            weather.h

FORMS    += mainwindow.ui
```

Now, we can write the `Weather` class. Its `weather.h` header file is pasted as follows:

```
#ifndef WEATHER_H
#define WEATHER_H

#include <QObject>
```

```
#include <QJsonDocument>
#include <QJsonObject>
#include <QNetworkAccessManager>
#include <QNetworkReply>
#include <QImage>

class Weather : public QObject
{
    Q_OBJECT
    public:
    explicit Weather(QObject *parent = 0);

    signals:
    void updateFinished(const QString &location, const QString
        &temp, const QString &wind);
    void imageDownloaded(const QImage &);

    public slots:
    void updateData(const QString &woeid);
    void getAttrImg();

    private:
    QNetworkAccessManager *naManager;
    QNetworkReply *imgReply;
    QImage attrImg;

    private slots:
    void onSSLErrors(QNetworkReply *);
    void onQueryFinished(QNetworkReply *);
};

#endif // WEATHER_H
```

In addition to the weather information query, we also use this class to get an attribution image, which is stated in the Yahoo! documentation. It is kind of trivial in traditional Qt/C++ that we have to use QNetworkAccessManager to access QUrl, because QJsonDocument cannot load from QUrl directly. Anyway, let's see how we get the result from the Yahoo! Weather API in the weather.cpp file. The header part includes the following lines:

```
#include <QDebug>
#include <QNetworkRequest>
#include <QJsonArray>
#include "weather.h"
```

Then, let's see the constructor of `Weather`. Here, we simply construct the `QNetworkAccessManager` object, `naManager`, and connect its signals:

```
Weather::Weather(QObject *parent) :
    QObject(parent)
{
    naManager = new QNetworkAccessManager(this);

    connect(naManager, &QNetworkAccessManager::finished, this,
        &Weather::onQueryFinished);
    connect(naManager, &QNetworkAccessManager::sslErrors, this,
        &Weather::onSSLErrors);
}
```

The `onSSLErrors` slot is simply to let the `QNetworkReply` object ignore all the SSL errors. This won't cause any serious problems in this case. However, if you're dealing with a secure communication or anything else that needs to validate the connection, you may wish to look into the error.

```
void Weather::onSSLErrors(QNetworkReply *re)
{
    re->ignoreSslErrors();
}
```

Then, let's check the `updateData` function before `onQueryFinished`. Here, we construct `QUrl`, which is the Yahoo! Weather API's exact address. Note that you don't need to use an HTML code for `QUrl`. In fact, it'd be better to use a space along with the other symbols directly. After this, similar to the previous chapter, we use `QNetworkRequest` to wrap this `QUrl` and dispatch the request through `QNetworkAccessManager`.

```
void Weather::updateData(const QString &woeid)
{
    QUrl url("https://query.yahooapis.com/v1/public/yql?q=select *
        from weather.forecast where woeid = " + woeid +
            "&format=json");
    QNetworkRequest req(url);
    naManager->get(req);
}
```

As for the `getAttrImg` function, it's almost the same. The only difference is that this function is used to get an attribution image instead of weather information. We store the reply as `imgReply` so that we can distinguish the image from the weather.

```
void Weather::getAttrImg()
{
    QUrl url("https://poweredby.yahoo.com/purple.png");
    QNetworkRequest req(url);
    imgReply = naManager->get(req);
}
```

If the corresponding `QNetworkReply` object is finished, the `onQueryFinished` slot function will be executed, which is shown in the following code. After all the pavement, let's see what's inside this function. We can check whether there is any error in the reply at the very beginning. Then, if it's `imgReply`, we cook `QImage` from the data and emit a signal to send this image out. If none of these happen, we'll parse the weather from the JSON reply.

```
void Weather::onQueryFinished(QNetworkReply *re)
{
    if (re->error() != QNetworkReply::NoError) {
        qDebug() << re->errorString();
        re->deleteLater();
        return;
    }

    if (re == imgReply) {
        attrImg = QImage::fromData(imgReply->readAll());
        emit imageDownloaded(attrImg);
        imgReply->deleteLater();
        return;
    }

    QByteArray result = re->readAll();
    re->deleteLater();

    QJsonParseError err;
    QJsonDocument doc = QJsonDocument::fromJson(result, &err);
    if (err.error != QJsonParseError::NoError) {
        qDebug() << err.errorString();
        return;
    }
```

```cpp
    QJsonObject obj = doc.object();
    QJsonObject res =
        obj.value("query").toObject().value("results").toObject().
            value("channel").toObject();

    QJsonObject locObj = res["location"].toObject();
    QString location;
    for(QJsonObject::ConstIterator it = locObj.constBegin(); it !=
        locObj.constEnd(); ++it) {
        location.append((*it).toString());
        if ((it + 1) != locObj.constEnd()) {
            location.append(", ");
        }
    }

    QString temperature =
        res["item"].toObject()["condition"].toObject()["temp"].
            toString() +
                res["units"].toObject()["temperature"].toString();

    QJsonObject windObj = res["wind"].toObject();
    QString wind;
    for(QJsonObject::ConstIterator it = windObj.constBegin(); it
        != windObj.constEnd(); ++it) {
        wind.append(it.key());
        wind.append(": ");
        wind.append((*it).toString());
        wind.append("\n");
    }

    emit updateFinished(location, temperature, wind);
}
```

As I mentioned before, it is trivial. First, we read the result from `QNetworkReply`, and then use `QJsonDocument::fromJson` to parse the `byte` array as a JSON document. If there is an error during the process, we simply print the error string and return. Then, we need to get `QJsonObject` contained in `QJsonDocument`. Only then can we parse all the information inside it. The formatted result using `560743` as the WOEID is shown as follows:

```json
{
  "query":{
    "count":1,
    "created":"2014-12-05T23:19:54Z",
    "lang":"en-GB",
```

```
"results":{
  "channel":{
    "title":"Yahoo! Weather - Dublin, IE",
    "link":"http://us.rd.yahoo.com/dailynews/rss/weather/
      Dublin__IE/*http://weather.yahoo.com/forecast/
        EIXX0014_f.html",
    "description":"Yahoo! Weather for Dublin, IE",
    "language":"en-us",
    "lastBuildDate":"Fri, 05 Dec 2014 9:59 pm GMT",
    "ttl":"60",
    "location":{
      "city":"Dublin",
      "country":"Ireland",
      "region":"DUB"
    },
    "units":{
      "distance":"mi",
      "pressure":"in",
      "speed":"mph",
      "temperature":"F"
    },
    "wind":{
      "chill":"29",
      "direction":"230",
      "speed":"8"
    },
    "atmosphere":{
      "humidity":"93",
      "pressure":"30.36",
      "rising":"1",
      "visibility":"6.21"
    },
    "astronomy":{
      "sunrise":"8:22 am",
      "sunset":"4:09 pm"
    },
    "image":{
      "title":"Yahoo! Weather",
      "width":"142",
      "height":"18",
      "link":"http://weather.yahoo.com",
      "url":"http://l.yimg.com/a/i/brand/purplelogo//uh/us/
        news-wea.gif"
    },
```

```
"item":{
  "title":"Conditions for Dublin, IE at 9:59 pm GMT",
  "lat":"53.33",
  "long":"-6.29",
  "link":"http://us.rd.yahoo.com/dailynews/rss/weather/
    Dublin__IE/*http://weather.yahoo.com/forecast/
      EIXX0014_f.html",
  "pubDate":"Fri, 05 Dec 2014 9:59 pm GMT",
  "condition":{
    "code":"29",
    "date":"Fri, 05 Dec 2014 9:59 pm GMT",
    "temp":"36",
    "text":"Partly Cloudy"
  },
  "description":"\n<img src=\"http://l.yimg.com/a/i/us/we/
    52/29.gif\"/><br />\n<b>Current Conditions:</b><br
      />\nPartly Cloudy, 36 F<BR />\n<BR /><b>Forecast:
        </b><BR />\nFri - Partly Cloudy. High: 44 Low:
          39<br />\nSat - Mostly Cloudy. High: 48 Low:
            41<br />\nSun - Mostly Sunny/Wind. High: 43
              Low: 37<br />\nMon - Mostly Sunny/Wind.
                High: 43 Low: 37<br />\nTue - PM Light
                  Rain/Wind. High: 52 Low: 38<br />\n<br
                    />\n<a href=\"http://us.rd.yahoo.com/
                      dailynews/rss/weather/Dublin__IE/
                        *http://weather.yahoo.com/
                          forecast/EIXX0014_f.html\">Full
                            Forecast at Yahoo! Weather
                              </a><BR/><BR/>\n(provided by
                                <a href=\"http://
                                  www.weather.com\" >The
                                    Weather Channel</a>)
                                      <br/>\n",
  "forecast":[
  {
    "code":"29",
    "date":"5 Dec 2014",
    "day":"Fri",
    "high":"44",
    "low":"39",
    "text":"Partly Cloudy"
  },
  {
    "code":"28",
    "date":"6 Dec 2014",
    "day":"Sat",
```

```json
        "high":"48",
        "low":"41",
        "text":"Mostly Cloudy"
      },
      {
        "code":"24",
        "date":"7 Dec 2014",
        "day":"Sun",
        "high":"43",
        "low":"37",
        "text":"Mostly Sunny/Wind"
      },
      {
        "code":"24",
        "date":"8 Dec 2014",
        "day":"Mon",
        "high":"43",
        "low":"37",
        "text":"Mostly Sunny/Wind"
      },
      {
        "code":"11",
        "date":"9 Dec 2014",
        "day":"Tue",
        "high":"52",
        "low":"38",
        "text":"PM Light Rain/Wind"
      }
      ],
      "guid":{
        "isPermaLink":"false",
        "content":"EIXX0014_2014_12_09_7_00_GMT"
      }
    }
   }
  }
 }
}
```

 For details about JSON, visit `http://www.json.org`.

As you can see, all the information is stored inside query/results/channel. Therefore, we need to convert it to QJsonObject, level by level. As you can see in the code, QJsonObject res is channel. Note that the value function will return a QJsonValue object and you will need to call toObject() to make it QJsonObject before you can use the value function to parse the value again. After this, it's pretty straightforward. The locObj object is the location where we use a for loop to put the values together, where as QJsonObject::ConstIterator is just Qt's wrapper of STL const_iterator.

To obtain the current temperature, we need to go through a similar journey to channel because the temperature is in item/condition/temp, while its unit is units/temperature.

As for the wind section, we use a lazy way to retrieve the data. The windObj line is not a single value statement; instead, it has several keys and values. Therefore, we use a for loop to walk through this array and retrieve both of its keys along with its value, and simply put them together.

Now, let's go back to the MainWindow class to see how to interact with the Weather class. The header file of MainWindow, which is mainwindow.h, is pasted here:

```
#ifndef MAINWINDOW_H
#define MAINWINDOW_H

#include <QMainWindow>
#include "weather.h"

namespace Ui {
  class MainWindow;
}

class MainWindow : public QMainWindow
{
  Q_OBJECT

public:
  explicit MainWindow(QWidget *parent = 0);
  ~MainWindow();

private:
  Ui::MainWindow *ui;
  Weather *w;
```

```
private slots:
  void onOkButtonClicked();
  void onAttrImageDownloaded(const QImage &);
  void onWeatherUpdateFinished(const QString &location, const
    QString &temp, const QString &wind);
};
```

```
#endif // MAINWINDOW_H
```

We declare a `Weather` object pointer, `w`, as the `MainWindow` class's private member.
Meanwhile, `onOkButtonClicked` is the handler when `okButton` gets clicked. The
`onAttrImageDownloaded` and `onWeatherUpdateFinished` functions will be coupled
with the `Weather` class's signals. Now, let's see what's inside the source file:

```
#include "mainwindow.h"
#include "ui_mainwindow.h"

MainWindow::MainWindow(QWidget *parent) :
  QMainWindow(parent),
  ui(new Ui::MainWindow)
{
  ui->setupUi(this);
  w = new Weather(this);

  connect(ui->okButton, &QPushButton::clicked, this,
    &MainWindow::onOkButtonClicked);
  connect(w, &Weather::updateFinished, this,
    &MainWindow::onWeatherUpdateFinished);
  connect(w, &Weather::imageDownloaded, this,
    &MainWindow::onAttrImageDownloaded);
  w->getAttrImg();
}

MainWindow::~MainWindow()
{
  delete ui;
}

void MainWindow::onOkButtonClicked()
{
  w->updateData(ui->woeidEdit->text());
}
```

```cpp
void MainWindow::onAttrImageDownloaded(const QImage &img)
{
  ui->attrLabel->setPixmap(QPixmap::fromImage(img));
}

void MainWindow::onWeatherUpdateFinished(const QString &location,
  const QString &temp, const QString &wind)
{
  ui->locationLabel->setText(location);
  ui->tempLabel->setText(temp);
  ui->windLabel->setText(wind);
}
```

In the constructor, apart from the signals connection and the w object's construction, we call getAttrImg of w to retrieve the attribution image. When the image is downloaded, the onAttrImageDownloaded slot function will be executed where the image will be displayed on attrLabel.

Once the user clicks on okButton, the onOkButtonClicked slot function gets executed, where we call the updateData function of the Weather class to pass the WOEID. Then, when the update is finished, the updateFinished signal is emitted and onWeatherUpdateFinished is executed. We just use these three QString objects to set the corresponding label's text.

Now, test your application to see if it's running as shown in this screenshot:

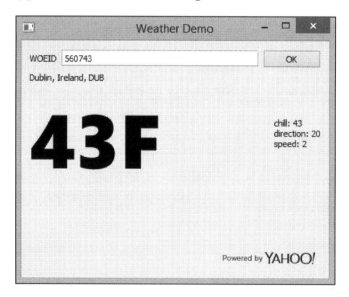

Parsing XML results

Although a lot of APIs provide both XML and JSON results, you may still find that some of them only offer one format. Besides, you might feel that parsing JSON in C++/Qt is not a pleasant process. You may remember how easy it is to parse the XML model in QML/Qt Quick. Well, let's see how to do this in C++/Qt.

To make use of an `xml` module, we have to add `xml` to QT in the `project` file, the same way we did to network. This time, Qt has provided an XML reader class called `QXmlStreamReader` to help us parse the XML documents. The first thing we need to do is to change the `updateData` function in the `Weather` class to let the Yahoo! Weather API return an XML result.

```
void Weather::updateData(const QString &woeid)
{
  QUrl url("https://query.yahooapis.com/v1/public/yql?q=select *
    from weather.forecast where woeid = " + woeid +
      "&format=xml");
    QNetworkRequest req(url);
    naManager->get(req);
}
```

The changing of `&format=json` to `&format=xml` needs to be done here. In contrast to this, there is a lot of work to do in the `onQueryFinished` slot function. The old JSON part is commented out so that we can write the XML parsing code. The modified function without the comment is shown as follows:

```
void Weather::onQueryFinished(QNetworkReply *re)
{
  if (re->error() != QNetworkReply::NoError) {
    qDebug() << re->errorString();
    re->deleteLater();
    return;
  }

  if (re == imgReply) {
    attrImg = QImage::fromData(imgReply->readAll());
    emit imageDownloaded(attrImg);
    imgReply->deleteLater();
    return;
  }

  QByteArray result = re->readAll();
  re->deleteLater();
```

```
QXmlStreamReader xmlReader(result);
while (!xmlReader.atEnd() && !xmlReader.hasError()) {
  QXmlStreamReader::TokenType token = xmlReader.readNext();
  if (token == QXmlStreamReader::StartElement) {
    QStringRef name = xmlReader.name();
    if (name == "channel") {
      parseXMLChannel(xmlReader);
    }
  }
}
}
```

Here, `parseXMLChannel` is a newly created member function. We can use a separate function to make our code neat and tidy.

 Remember to declare the `parseXMLChannel` function in the header file.

Its definition is pasted as follows:

```
void Weather::parseXMLChannel(QXmlStreamReader &xml)
{
  QString location, temperature, wind;
  QXmlStreamReader::TokenType token = xml.readNext();
  while (token != QXmlStreamReader::EndDocument) {
    if (token == QXmlStreamReader::EndElement ||
      xml.name().isEmpty()) {
      token = xml.readNext();
      continue;
    }

    QStringRef name = xml.name();
    if (name == "location") {
      QXmlStreamAttributes locAttr = xml.attributes();
      location = locAttr.value("city").toString() + ", " +
        locAttr.value("country").toString() + ", " +
          locAttr.value("region").toString();
    }
```

```
    else if (name == "units") {
      temperature =
        xml.attributes().value("temperature").toString();
    }
    else if (name == "wind") {
      QXmlStreamAttributes windAttr = xml.attributes();
      for (QXmlStreamAttributes::ConstIterator it =
        windAttr.begin(); it != windAttr.end(); ++it) {
        wind.append(it->name().toString());
        wind.append(": ");
        wind.append(it->value());
        wind.append("\n");
      }
    }
    else if (name == "condition") {
      temperature.prepend
        (xml.attributes().value("temp").toString());
      break;//we got all information, exit the loop
    }
    token = xml.readNext();
  }

  emit updateFinished(location, temperature, wind);
}
```

Before we walk through `parseXMLChannel` function, I'd like to show you what the XML document looks like, shown as follows:

```
<?xml version="1.0"?>
<query xmlns:yahoo="http://www.yahooapis.com/v1/base.rng"
  yahoo:count="1" yahoo:created="2014-12-06T22:50:22Z"
    yahoo:lang="en-GB">
  <results>
    <channel>
      <title>Yahoo! Weather - Dublin, IE</title>
      <link>
        http://us.rd.yahoo.com/dailynews/rss/weather/Dublin__IE/*
          http://weather.yahoo.com/forecast/EIXX0014_f.html</link>
      <description>Yahoo! Weather for Dublin, IE</description>
      <language>en-us</language>
      <lastBuildDate>Sat, 06 Dec 2014 9:59 pm GMT</lastBuildDate>
      <ttl>60</ttl>
```

```xml
<yweather:location xmlns:
  yweather="http://xml.weather.yahoo.com/ns/rss/1.0"
    city="Dublin" country="Ireland" region="DUB"/>
<yweather:units xmlns:
  yweather="http://xml.weather.yahoo.com/ns/rss/1.0"
    distance="mi" pressure="in" speed="mph"
      temperature="F"/>
<yweather:wind xmlns:
  yweather="http://xml.weather.yahoo.com/ns/rss/1.0"
    chill="41" direction="230" speed="22"/>
<yweather:atmosphere xmlns:
  yweather="http://xml.weather.yahoo.com/ns/rss/1.0"
    humidity="93" pressure="30.03" rising="2"
      visibility="6.21"/>
<yweather:astronomy xmlns:
  yweather="http://xml.weather.yahoo.com/ns/rss/1.0"
    sunrise="8:24 am" sunset="4:07 pm"/>
<image>
  <title>Yahoo! Weather</title>
  <width>142</width>
  <height>18</height>
  <link>http://weather.yahoo.com</link>
  <url>http://l.yimg.com/a/i/brand/purplelogo//uh/us/news-
    wea.gif</url>
</image>
<item>
  <title>Conditions for Dublin, IE at 9:59 pm GMT</title>
  <geo:lat xmlns:
    geo="http://www.w3.org/2003/01/geo/wgs84_pos#">53.33</
      geo:lat>
  <geo:long xmlns:
    geo="http://www.w3.org/2003/01/geo/
      wgs84_pos#">-6.29</geo:long>
  <link>
    http://us.rd.yahoo.com/dailynews/rss/weather/
      Dublin__IE/*http://weather.yahoo.com/forecast/
        EIXX0014_f.html</link>
  <pubDate>Sat, 06 Dec 2014 9:59 pm GMT</pubDate>
  <yweather:condition xmlns:
    yweather="http://xml.weather.yahoo.com/ns/rss/1.0"
      code="27" date="Sat, 06 Dec 2014 9:59 pm GMT"
        temp="48" text="Mostly Cloudy"/>
```

```
<description><![CDATA[<img src=
  "http://l.yimg.com/a/i/us/we/52/27.gif"/><br />
    <b>Current Conditions:</b><br /> Mostly Cloudy, 48
      F<BR /> <BR /><b>Forecast:</b><BR /> Sat - Light
        Rain/Wind Late. High: 48 Low: 42<br /> Sun -
          Mostly Sunny/Wind. High: 44 Low: 37<br /> Mon -
            Sunny. High: 43 Low: 37<br /> Tue -
              Showers/Wind. High: 53 Low: 39<br /> Wed -
                Partly Cloudy/Wind. High: 45 Low: 39<br />
                  <br /> <a
                    href="http://us.rd.yahoo.com/
                      dailynews/rss/weather/Dublin__IE/*
                        http://weather.yahoo.com/forecast/
                          EIXX0014_f.html">Full Forecast
                            at Yahoo! Weather</a><BR/>
                              <BR/> (provided by <a
                                href="http://
                                  www.weather.com" >The
                                    Weather Channel</a>)
                                      <br/>]]>
                                        </description>
<yweather:forecast xmlns:
  yweather="http://xml.weather.yahoo.com/ns/rss/1.0"
    code="11" date="6 Dec 2014" day="Sat" high="48"
      low="42" text="Light Rain/Wind Late"/>
<yweather:forecast xmlns:
  yweather="http://xml.weather.yahoo.com/ns/rss/1.0"
    code="24" date="7 Dec 2014" day="Sun" high="44"
      low="37" text="Mostly Sunny/Wind"/>
<yweather:forecast xmlns:
  yweather="http://xml.weather.yahoo.com/ns/rss/1.0"
    code="32" date="8 Dec 2014" day="Mon" high="43"
      low="37" text="Sunny"/>
<yweather:forecast xmlns:
  yweather="http://xml.weather.yahoo.com/ns/rss/1.0"
    code="11" date="9 Dec 2014" day="Tue" high="53"
      low="39" text="Showers/Wind"/>
<yweather:forecast xmlns:
  yweather="http://xml.weather.yahoo.com/ns/rss/1.0"
    code="24" date="10 Dec 2014" day="Wed" high="45"
      low="39" text="Partly Cloudy/Wind"/>
<guid isPermaLink="false">EIXX0014_2014_12_10_7_00_GMT
  </guid>
</item>
```

```
      </channel>
    </results>
  </query>
<!--  total: 27  -->
<!--  engine4.yql.bf1.yahoo.com  -->
```

As you can deduce, the XML structure shares a lot of similarities with the JSON document. For instance, all the data we need is still stored in query/results/channel. The difference is, however, more significant than you may have expected.

 If you want to learn XML thoroughly, check the XML tutorial at http://www.w3schools.com/xml/.

In the onQueryFinished slot, we use a while loop to let xmlReader keep reading until the end or until an error. The readNext function of the QXmlStreamReader class will read the next token and return its type. TokenType is an enum, which describes the type of token currently being read. Each time you call readNext, QXmlStreamReader will move forward by one token. If we want to read all the data of one element, we may have to read it from the beginning. Therefore, we use an if statement to ensure that the token is at the starting. In addition to this, we test if we're reading the channel now. Then, we call parseXMLChannel to retrieve all data that we need.

In the parseXMLChannel function, pretty much the same strategy is used. We test the name element so that we know which stage we are in. One thing worth your attention is that all prefixes such as yweather: are omitted. Hence, you should use location instead of yweather:location. Other parts are similar to their counterparts in JSON, where QStringRef is similar to QJsonValue. Last but not least, QXmlStreamReader is a stream reader, which means that it reads in order. In other words, we can break the while loop after we get temp in condition since condition is the last element that we're interested in.

After these changes, you can build and run this application again and you should expect it to run in the same manner.

Building Qt applications for Android

You may wonder how to build Qt applications for Android devices since this application is built for desktop PCs. Well, it's much easier than you thought.

1. Switch to **Projects** mode.

2. Click on **Add Kit** and select **Android for armeabit-v7a (GCC 4.9 and Qt 5.3.2)**. Note that the text may differ a little bit.

3. Plug in your phone if you're using it as the target Android device.

4. Open **Command Prompt** and run `adb devices`. Make sure your device is on the list.

Now, click on **Run** and Qt will prompt a dialog asking you to select the Android device, as shown in the following screenshot:

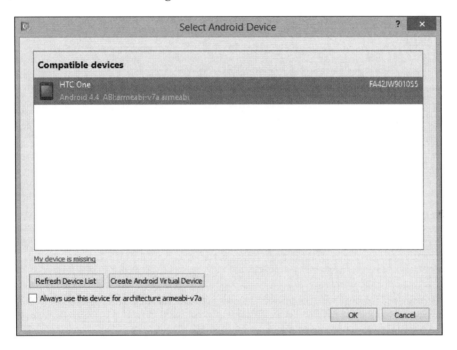

We choose to run our application on an actual Android device, which is an HTC One phone in this case. If you don't have any available Android devices, you may have to create a virtual device, as mentioned at the beginning of this chapter. For both the options, choose the device and click on the **OK** button.

 On an actual Android device, you need to go to **Settings** and turn on **USB debugging** in **Developer options**.

As you can see from the following screenshot, the demonstration runs well. It definitely needs ongoing improvements and UI optimization before submitting, though. However, remember that we designed and built this application for a desktop PC! We have just built it for a mobile phone without any modification and it runs as expected.

When you test the application, all the information is printed to the **Application Output** panel in Qt Creator. This could be useful when your application runs unexpectedly.

Parsing JSON in QML

Let's rewrite the weather demo in QML. You will find out how easy and elegant it is to write such an application in QML. Since the XML part is already covered in the previous chapter, we'll focus on parsing JSON this time.

First, create a new Qt Quick application project named `Weather_QML`. Keep the other settings as default, which means we use **Qt Quick Controls**. Remember to tick the checkbox of the Android kit.

Create a new QML file named `Weather.qml` to mimic the `Weather` class in the previous C++ code. This file is pasted here:

```
import QtQuick 2.3
import QtQuick.Controls 1.2

Rectangle {
  Column {
    anchors.fill: parent
    spacing: 6

    Label {
      id: location
      width: parent.width
      fontSizeMode: Text.Fit
      minimumPointSize: 9
      font.pointSize: 12
    }

    Row {
      spacing: 20
      width: parent.width
      height: parent.height

    Label {
      id: temp
      width: parent.width / 2
      height: parent.height
      fontSizeMode: Text.Fit
      minimumPointSize: 12
      font.pointSize: 72
      font.bold: true
    }
```

```
      Label {
        id: wind
        width: temp.width - 20
        height: parent.height
        fontSizeMode: Text.Fit
        minimumPointSize: 9
        font.pointSize: 24
      }
    }
  }

  Image {
    id: attrImg
    anchors { right: parent.right; bottom: parent.bottom }
    fillMode: Image.PreserveAspectFit
    source: 'https://poweredby.yahoo.com/purple.png'
  }

  function query (woeid) {
    var url = 'https://query.yahooapis.com/v1/public/yql?q=select
      * from weather.forecast where woeid = ' + woeid +
        '&format=json'
    var res
    var doc = new XMLHttpRequest()
    doc.onreadystatechange = function() {
      if (doc.readyState == XMLHttpRequest.DONE) {
        res = doc.responseText
        parseJSON(res)
      }
    }
    doc.open('GET', url, true)
    doc.send()
  }

  function parseJSON(data) {
    var obj = JSON.parse(data)

    if (typeof(obj) == 'object') {
      if (obj.hasOwnProperty('query')) {
        var ch = obj.query.results.channel
        var loc = '', win = ''
        for (var lk in ch.location) {
          loc += ch.location[lk] + ', '
        }
```

```
        for (var wk in ch.wind) {
          win += wk + ': ' + ch.wind[wk] + '\n'
        }
        location.text = loc
        temp.text = ch.item.condition.temp + ch.units.temperature
        wind.text = win
      }
    }
  }
}
```

The first part is just a QML version UI of the previous application. You may want to pay attention to the `fontSizeMode` and `minimumPointSize` property in `Label`. These properties are newly introduced in Qt 5, and enable the text scale to be dynamically adjusted. By setting `Text.Fit` as `fontSizeMode`, it'll shrink the text if `height` or `width` is not sufficient for the text, where `minimumPointSize` is the minimum point size. The text will get elided if it can't display at a minimum size. Similar to the `elide` property, you have to explicitly set the `width` and `height` property of `Text` or `Label` to make this dynamic mechanism work.

The attribution image is displayed in a slightly different way from C++. We utilize the flexibility of Qt Quick to float `Image` on top of the whole item by setting only `anchors`. In addition to this, we don't need to use `QNetworkAccessManager` to download the image. It's all in one.

After the UI part, we create the two JavaScript functions to do the dirty work. The `query` function is used to send an `http` request and pass the received data to the `parseJSON` function once it's done. Don't get confused by XML in `XMLHttpRequest`; it's just a traditional naming convention. Then, we create a `handler` function for `onreadystatechanged`, which is to call `parseJSON` when the request is done. Note that the `open` function won't send the request, only the `send` function does.

It's still short and clean in the `parseJSON` function. `JSON.parse` will return a `JSON` object if it is parsed successfully. Therefore, we need to test whether its type is `object` before we get into parsing. Then, we just do one more test to see whether it has `query` as its property. If so, we can start extracting data from `obj`. Unlike its C++ counterpart, we can treat all its keys as its properties and use the `dot` operation to access them directly. To shorten the operations, we first create a `ch` variable, which is `query/results/channel`. Next, we extract the data from the `ch` object. Finally, we change the text directly.

> The `ch.location` and `ch.wind` objects can be treated as `QVariantMap` objects. Thus, we can use the `for` loop to easily extract the values.

Let's edit the `main.qml` file as shown here:

```
import QtQuick 2.3
import QtQuick.Controls 1.2
import "qrc:/"

ApplicationWindow {
  visible: true
  width: 240
  height: 320
  title: qsTr("Weather QML")

  Row {
    id: inputField
    anchors { top: parent.top; topMargin: 10; left: parent.left;
      leftMargin: 10; right: parent.right; rightMargin: 10 }
    spacing: 6

    Label {
      id: woeidLabel
      text: "WOEID"
    }
    TextField {
      width: inputField.width - woeidLabel.width
      inputMethodHints: Qt.ImhDigitsOnly
      onAccepted: weather.query(text)
    }
  }

  Weather {
    anchors { top: inputField.bottom; topMargin: 10; left:
      parent.left; leftMargin: 10; right: parent.right;
        rightMargin: 10; bottom: parent.bottom; bottomMargin: 10 }
    id: weather
  }
}
```

`Row` is the same WOEID input panel, for which we don't create an **OK** button this time. Instead, we handle the accepted signal in `onAccepted` by calling the `query` function in `weather`, which is a `Weather` element. We set the `inputMethodHints` property to `Qt.ImhDigitsOnly`, which is useful on mobile platforms. This application should run almost the same as the C++ one or should we say better.

The `inputMethodHints` property may seem useless on a desktop; indeed, you need to use `inputMask` and `validator` to restrict the acceptable input. However, it shows its power on mobiles, as follows:

As you can see, `inputMethodHints` not only restricts the input, but it also provides a better experience for users. This is also viable in a C++/Qt development; you can find the relevant functions to achieve this. The whole point in QML is that parsing the JSON and XML documents is easier and tidier than C++.

Summary

After this chapter, you're expected to handle common tasks and write types of real-world applications. You'll get your own understanding of Qt Quick and traditional Qt. It's also a current trend to write hybrid applications, which make full use of both of them by writing the C++ plugins to enhance QML. QML has an unbeatable advantage of flexible UI design, which is even more obvious on mobile platforms. While the development part is nearing the end, in the next chapter we'll talk about how to support multiple languages.

8
Enabling Your Qt Application to Support Other Languages

In this era of globalization, the internationalization and localization of applications is almost inevitable. Fortunately, Qt provides relevant classes, along with some handy tools such as **Qt Linguist** to ease the burden of developers and translators. In this chapter, we will use two example applications to demonstrate the following topics:

- Internationalization of Qt applications
- Translating Qt Widgets applications
- Disambiguating identical texts
- Changing languages dynamically
- Translating Qt Quick applications

Internationalization of Qt applications

Internationalization and localization are the processes of adapting the application to other locales, which might include different languages and regional differences. In software development, internationalization refers to designing an application in such a way that it can be adapted to various languages and regions without code changes. On the other hand, localization means adapting internationalized software for a specific language or region. This usually involves locale-specific components and translating text.

Qt has done a lot to free developers from different writing systems. We don't need to worry about how different languages display and input, as long as we use Qt's input and display controls or their subclasses.

In most cases, what we need to do is to produce translations and enable them in the application. Qt offers the QTranslator class, which loads the translation file and displays the corresponding language on the screen. The procedure is concluded in the following diagram:

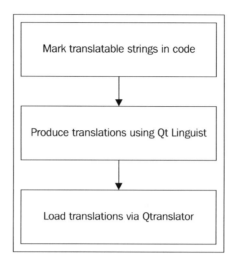

First of all, Qt won't just make all the strings translatable, because that would obviously be a disaster. Instead, you need to explicitly set whether the string is translatable in code or in the **Design** mode. In the Qt/C++ code, use the tr() function to enclose all the strings that can be translated. We use the qsTr() function to do this job in the Qt Quick/QML code. Let me show you an example. Here is a demonstration of the normal usage of a string:

```
qDebug() << "Hello World";
```

This will output Hello World to the standard output stream, which is your command prompt or shell in general cases. If we want to make Hello World translatable, we need to use a tr() function to enclose the string, as follows:

```
qDebug() << tr("Hello World");
```

Since tr() is a static public member function of the QObject class, you can still use it even for a non QObject class.

```
qDebug() << QObject::tr("Hello World");
```

Then, we need to use the `lupdate` command, which is located in **Tools | External | Linguist | Update Translations (lupdate)** in Qt Creator. This will update, or create if the **translation source (TS)** file doesn't exist. You can then use Qt Linguist to translate the strings. Before you release your application, run the `lrelease` command, which is located in **Tools | External | Linguist | Release Translations (lrelease)**, to generate the **Qt message (QM)** files that can be loaded by an application dynamically. Don't worry if it confuses you; we'll use two examples to walk you through these procedures.

Translating Qt Widgets applications

First, let's create a new Qt Widget project, whose name is `Internationalization`. Then, edit `mainwindow.ui` in the **Design** mode.

1. As usual, remove the status bar, menu bar, and tool bar.
2. Add **Label** into `centralWidget` and change its object name to `nonTransLabel`. Then, change its text to `This is a non-translatable label` and uncheck `translatable` under `text` in **Property Editor**.
3. Drag a **Push Button** just beneath `nonTransLabel` with `transButton` as its object name. Change its text to `This is a translatable button`.
4. Change **Lay out** to **Lay Out Vertically** in **MainWindow**.
5. Resize the frame to a comfortable size.

Go back to editing the `Internationalization.pro` project file in the **Edit** mode. Add a line indicating the translation source file, which is shown as follows:

```
TRANSLATIONS = Internationalization_de.ts
```

The `_de` suffix is a locale code, indicating that this is a German translation source file. The locale codes are defined by **Internet Engineering Task Force** in the **BCP 47** document series. Historically, Qt follows the POSIX definition, which is slightly different from BCP 47. In this, it uses underscores (_) instead of hyphens (-) to separate subtags. In other words, Brazilian Portuguese is expressed as `pt_BR` instead of `pt-BR`. Meanwhile, Qt has provided some APIs to conform the locale name to a BCP 47 definition since the Qt 4.8 version.

To ensure this change is valid, save the project file and right-click on the project and select **Run qmake**. After this, we can generate the translation source file, which is exactly `Internationalization_de.ts`, by executing the `lupdate` command. The results will be printed in the **General Messages** panel, which contains the strings added to the TS file, as shown here:

```
Updating 'Internationalization_de.ts'...
Found 3 source text(s) (3 new and 0 already existing)
```

Now, open the `Internationalization_de.ts` file in Qt Linguist. The overview UI of Qt Linguist is displayed in the following screenshot:

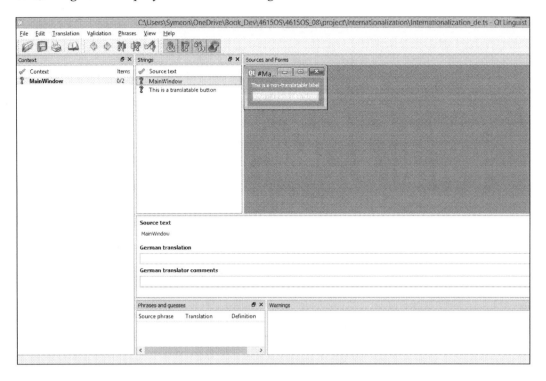

Context lists the source text context, which is the class name in most cases, while **Strings** contains all the translatable strings. **Sources and Forms** displays the corresponding location of the string, either as a piece of code or a UI form. Beneath them is the translation area, which lets you input the translation and comments, if there are any.

In addition to the overview, the icon in front of each entry is noteworthy. A yellow question mark (**?**) simply means there is no translation currently, while a green checkmark means accepted/correct, and a yellow checkmark stands for accepted/ warnings. You may also encounter a red exclamation mark (**!**), which indicates warnings. The sharp symbol (**#**) in front of a button's text in the **Sources and Forms** pane indicates untranslated, and possibly translatable, strings. Qt Linguist checks string translations automatically according to its own algorithm, which means that it may give a false warning. In this case, simply ignore the warning and accept the translation.

You'll find that the label text isn't among **Source text**. This is because we unchecked the `translatable` property. Now, input German translations in the translation area and click on the **Done and Next** button in the tool bar, then navigate to **Translation | Done and Next**. Or, even quicker, press *Ctrl + Enter* to accept the translation. When you've finished, click on the **Save** button, and then exit Qt Linguist.

Although it's recommended to use Qt Linguist for translation tasks, it's viable to use a normal text editor to edit the TS file directly. The TS file is XML-formatted and should be supported well by other editors.

After translating, return to Qt Creator and run the `lrelease` command to generate the `Internationalization_de.qm` file. At the current stage, your project folder should contain both the TS and QM files, as shown in the following screenshot:

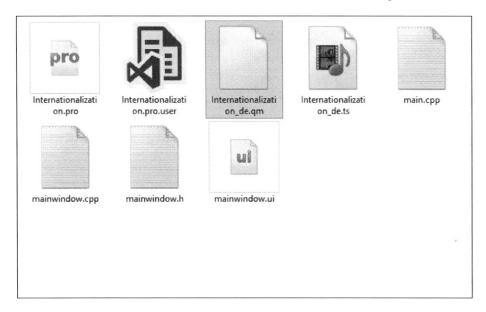

 Note that file icons may differ slightly on your computers because of different operating system and (or) software installations.

We already produced the QM file; it's now time to modify the `main.cpp` file in order to load the translation into this application.

```cpp
#include "mainwindow.h"
#include <QApplication>
#include <QTranslator>

int main(int argc, char *argv[])
{
  QApplication a(argc, argv);

  QTranslator translator;
  translator.load(QLocale::German, "Internationalization", "_");
  a.installTranslator(&translator);

  MainWindow w;
  w.show();

  return a.exec();
}
```

Here, `QTranslator` is used to load the German translation. Before we install translator into `QApplication`, we have to load a QM file by calling the `load` function. This will load the translation file whose filename consists of `Internationalization` followed by _ and the UI language name (which is `de` in this case) and `.qm` (the default value). There is a simplified overloaded `load` function. Our equivalent is as follows:

```cpp
translator.load("Internationalization_de");
```

Usually, it would be better to call the previous `load` function because it uses `QLocale::uiLanguages()`, and it will also format dates and numbers if they're necessary for the new locale. Whichever you choose, always remember that if you load the translation after the `MainWindow w;` line, `MainWindow` won't be able to use the translation at all.

If you run the application now, the application won't display German yet. Why? This is simply because `QTranslator` can't find the `Internationalization_de.qm` file. There are lots of ways to solve this problem. The neatest way is to change the working directory, while running the application in Qt Creator.

1. Switch to the **Projects** mode.
2. Switch to **Run Settings**.
3. Change **Working directory** to your project source directory where you put the `Internationalization_de.qm` file.

Now, run it again; you'll see German text on the screen, as follows:

The label is displayed in English as we expected, whereas the window title and button text are displayed in German.

You may think this solution pointless, since the German translation is loaded despite the system locale setting. Well, the application can load the translation according to the system locale with only one modification; that is, changing the translator load line to the one shown here:

```
translator.load(QLocale::system().language(),
    "Internationalization", "_");
```

Here, `system()` is a static member function of the `QLocale` class, which returns a `QLocale` object that initialized with the system locale. We then call the `language()` function to get the language of the current locale.

Disambiguating identical texts

If there are identical texts, the default behavior is to treat them as the texts with the same meaning. This could effectively save translators from translating the same texts. Meanwhile, this doesn't hold true all the time. For instance, the word open can be used as a noun or an adjective, which may be different words in other languages. Thankfully, it's possible and easy to disambiguate identical texts in Qt.

Now, let's add a `PushButton` and `openButton` between `transButton` and `nonTransLabel`. Use `Open` as its text, and then edit `mainwindow.h`. Add a new private slot named `onOpenButtonClicked()`, which is used to handle the event when `openButton` gets clicked. The relevant source file, `mainwindow.cpp`, is pasted as follows:

```
#include <QMessageBox>
#include "mainwindow.h"
#include "ui_mainwindow.h"
```

```
MainWindow::MainWindow(QWidget *parent) :
  QMainWindow(parent),
  ui(new Ui::MainWindow)
{
  ui->setupUi(this);

  connect(ui->openButton, &QPushButton::clicked, this,
    &MainWindow::onOpenButtonClicked);
}

MainWindow::~MainWindow()
{
  delete ui;
}

void MainWindow::onOpenButtonClicked()
{
  QMessageBox::information(this, tr("Dialog"), tr("Open"));
}
```

First, we connect the clicked signal of `openButton` to the `onOpenButtonClicked` slot of `MainWindow` in the constructor of `MainWindow`. Then, we simply use the static member function, `information`, of `QMessageBox` to pop-up an information dialog, using `Dialog` as the title and `Open` as its context. Don't forget to use the `tr()` function to make these strings translatable.

Now, run `lupdate` and open the TS file in Qt Linguist. There is only one **Open** string in the **Strings** panel, as shown here:

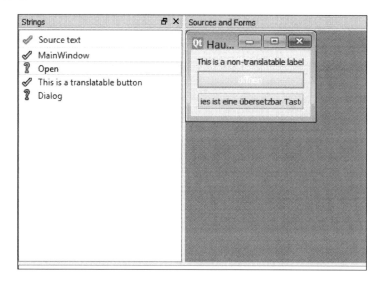

However, **Open** in the information dialog is supposed to have an adjective, which shouldn't be mixed up with the text in openButton. It's a comment that we need to separate this **Open** from the other Open. Modify the onOpenButtonClicked function in mainwindow.cpp:

```
void MainWindow::onOpenButtonClicked()
{
  QMessageBox::information(this, tr("Dialog"), tr("Open",
    "adj."));
}
```

Here, the second argument of the tr() function is the comment. Different comments stand for different texts. In this way, lupdate will treat them as nonidentical texts. Rerun lupdate, and you're able to translate two Open strings in Qt Linguist. The **Developer comments** column in the translation area is shown here. Qt Linguist will also show two translatable Open strings.

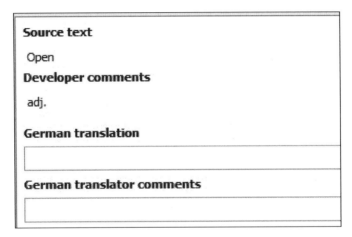

The equivalent property in the **Design** mode for openButton is disambiguation under the text property. After translation, execute lrelease, and then rerun the application and the two Open strings should have two different translations, which is demonstrated here:

Changing languages dynamically

Sometimes, people want to use languages other than the one specified by the system locale. This is a matter of application of the customized settings. This usually means restarting the application in order to load the corresponding translation file. This is partly because changing the language dynamically requires additional work. However, it's feasible and can be done with some lines. What's more important is that it delivers a better user experience!

Let's add a new `push` button to `MainWindow`. Name it `loadButton` and change its text to `Load/Unload Translation`. Then, edit the `main.cpp` file in the **Edit** mode. Remove all `QTranslator` related lines, as we'll be implementing this dynamic language switch in the `MainWindow` class. The `main.cpp` file should look like the originally generated one as follows:

```cpp
#include "mainwindow.h"
#include <QApplication>

int main(int argc, char *argv[])
{
  QApplication a(argc, argv);
  MainWindow w;
  w.show();

  return a.exec();
}
```

Now, edit `mainwindow.h`, as we need to declare some members here:

```cpp
#ifndef MAINWINDOW_H
#define MAINWINDOW_H

#include <QMainWindow>
#include <QTranslator>

namespace Ui {
class MainWindow;
}

class MainWindow : public QMainWindow
{
  Q_OBJECT
```

```
public:
  explicit MainWindow(QWidget *parent = 0);
  ~MainWindow();

private:
  Ui::MainWindow *ui;
  QTranslator *deTranslator;
  bool deLoaded;

private slots:
  void onOpenButtonClicked();
  void onLoadButtonClicked();

protected:
  void changeEvent(QEvent *);
};


#endif // MAINWINDOW_H
```

As you can tell, we moved QTranslator here, named it deTranslator, and used it as a pointer with the deLoaded variable to suggest whether or not we've already loaded the German translation. The following onLoadButtonClicked is a private slot function, which will be connected to the clicked signal of loadButton. Last but not least, we reimplement changeEvent, so that we can translate the entire user interface on the fly. It'll be clear in the mainwindow.cpp source file, where it is pasted as follows:

```
#include <QMessageBox>
#include "mainwindow.h"
#include "ui_mainwindow.h"

MainWindow::MainWindow(QWidget *parent) :
  QMainWindow(parent),
  ui(new Ui::MainWindow)
{
  ui->setupUi(this);

  deTranslator = new QTranslator(this);
  deTranslator->load(QLocale::German, "Internationalization",
    "_");
  deLoaded = false;

  connect(ui->openButton, &QPushButton::clicked, this,
    &MainWindow::onOpenButtonClicked);
```

```
    connect(ui->loadButton, &QPushButton::clicked, this,
       &MainWindow::onLoadButtonClicked);
}

MainWindow::~MainWindow()
{
   delete ui;
}

void MainWindow::onOpenButtonClicked()
{
   QMessageBox::information(this, tr("Dialog"), tr("Open",
      "adj."));
}

void MainWindow::onLoadButtonClicked()
{
   if (deLoaded) {
     deLoaded = false;
     qApp->removeTranslator(deTranslator);
   }
   else {
     deLoaded = true;
     qApp->installTranslator(deTranslator);
   }
}

void MainWindow::changeEvent(QEvent *e)
{
   if (e->type() == QEvent::LanguageChange) {
     ui->retranslateUi(this);
   }
   else {
     QMainWindow::changeEvent(e);
   }
}
```

In the constructor, we initialize deTranslator and load the German translation,
which is almost identical to what we did in main.cpp before. Then, we set deLoaded
to false, indicating that the German translation is not installed yet. Next, this is
followed by a connect statement.

Now, let's look into the `onLoadButtonClicked` function to see what will happen if the `loadButton` gets clicked. We set `deLoaded` to `false` and remove `deTranslator` if it's already loaded. Otherwise, we install `deTranslator` and set `deLoaded` to `true`. Remember that `qApp` is a predefined macro that simply refers to the current instance of `QCoreApplication`. Both `installTranslator` and `removeTranslator` will propagate the event to all the top-level windows, that is to say, `changeEvent` of `MainWindow` will be triggered in this case.

In order to update all the text according to the translator, we have to `reimplement` `changeEvent`. In this `reimplemented` function, we call the `retranslateUi` function to retranslate `MainWindow` if the event is `languageChange`. Otherwise, we simply call the inherited and default `QMainWindow::changeEvent` function.

When you firstly start the application, it'll display English text.

Once you click on the **Load/Unload Translation** button, all translatable and translated text will show in German.

It'll display in English if you click the button again. In addition to a nontranslatable label, `loadButton` will not be not translated either. This is because we didn't translate the button at all. However, as you can see, the lack of some translations won't prevent the application from loading other translated texts.

Translating Qt Quick applications

The procedure of translating a Qt Quick application is similar to a Qt Widgets application. We'll walk through the process with another example application.

Create a new Qt Quick application project and name it `Internationalization_QML`. The generated `main.qml` file has already added a `qsTr()` function for us. The contents may differ slightly in a later version of Qt Creator and (or) Qt Library. However, it should look similar to this one:

```qml
import QtQuick 2.3
import QtQuick.Controls 1.2

ApplicationWindow {
  visible: true
  width: 640
  height: 480
  title: qsTr("Hello World")

  menuBar: MenuBar {
    Menu {
      title: qsTr("File")
      MenuItem {
        text: qsTr("&Open")
        onTriggered: console.log("Open action triggered");
      }
      MenuItem {
        text: qsTr("Exit")
        onTriggered: Qt.quit();
      }
    }
  }

  Text {
    text: qsTr("Hello World")
    anchors.centerIn: parent
  }
}
```

Now, let's edit the `Internationalization_QML.pro` project file, whose modified version is pasted as follows:

```
TEMPLATE = app

QT += qml quick widgets

SOURCES += main.cpp

RESOURCES += qml.qrc

lupdate_only {
   SOURCES += main.qml
}

TRANSLATIONS = Internationalization_QML_de.ts

# Additional import path used to resolve QML modules in Qt
# Creator's code model
QML_IMPORT_PATH =

# Default rules for deployment.
include(deployment.pri)
```

In addition to the TRANSLATIONS line, we also add a `lupdate_only` block. It is crucial in this case.

 We probably don't need this block in the Qt/C++ projects because the `lupdate` tool extracts the translatable strings from SOURCES, HEADERS, and FORMS.

However, this means that all the strings located elsewhere won't be found, not even saying translating. On the other hand, the `qml` files are not the C++ source files that are going to be compiled by the C++ compiler. In this case, we use `lupdate_only` to restrict those SOURCES, which are only available for `lupdate`.

Now, executing `lupdate` can generate the translation source file for us. Similarly, we use Qt Linguist to translate the `Internationalization_QML_de.ts` file. Then, execute `lrelease` to generate the QM file.

To load the translation, we need to modify main.cpp into the one shown here:

```cpp
#include <QApplication>
#include <QQmlApplicationEngine>
#include <QTranslator>

int main(int argc, char *argv[])
{
  QApplication app(argc, argv);

  QTranslator translator;
  translator.load(QLocale::German, "Internationalization_QML", "_");
  app.installTranslator(&translator);

  QQmlApplicationEngine engine;
  engine.load(QUrl(QStringLiteral("qrc:/main.qml")));

  return app.exec();
}
```

Also, we need to change **Working directory** to this project's directory in **Run Settings** in the **Projects** mode. Now, run the application again; we should be able to see German text on the screen, as we can in the following screenshot:

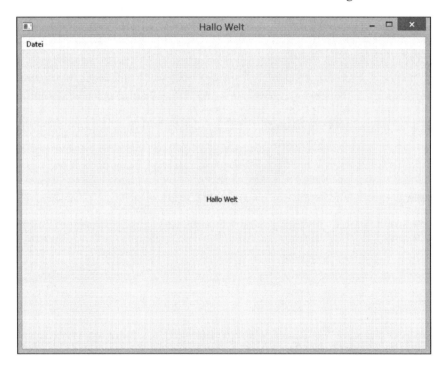

There is an alternative way to load the translations file, which doesn't need to change **Working directory**. Firstly, change the `translator.load` line in `main.cpp` to the following one:

```
translator.load(QLocale::German, "Internationalization_QML", "_",
    ":/");
```

We specify the directory that the translator should search. In this case, it's `":/"`, which is the top directory inside **Resources**. Please don't prepend `qrc` to the directory string; this will cause `translator` to be unable to find the QM file. A colon (`:`) is sufficient here to indicate that there is a `qrc` path inside **Resources**.

You can either create a new `qrc` file, or similar to what we do, add `Internationalization_QML_de.qm` to the current `qml.qrc` file.

1. Right-click on the `qml.qrc` file under **Resources** in **Projects Editor**.
2. Select **Open** in **Editor**.
3. Navigate to **Add | Add Files** on the lower-right panel.
4. Select the `Internationalization_QML_de.qm` file and click on **Open**.

Now, the `Internationalization_QML_de.qm` file should display on both **Editor** and the **Projects** tree like the following screenshot:

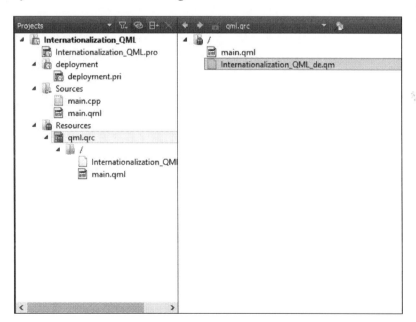

Go to the **Projects** mode and reset **Working directory** in **Run Settings**. Then, run the application again; the German translation should still load successfully.

So far, there is no huge difference between Qt and Qt Quick. However, it's tedious to achieve dynamic translation installation and removal in Qt Quick. You have to write a C++ class that installs and remove the translator, which then emits a signal indicating that there is a change to the text. Therefore, the best practice for the Qt Quick application is to make language a setting. The user can then load different translations. It needs a restart of the application, though.

Summary

You're now able to make your application more competitive by adding support for other languages now. Besides, the super easy to use Qt Linguist, which is also a cross-platform tool provided by Qt, is also covered in this chapter. In addition to the skills you learnt, you can also tell that Qt/C++ still holds a great advantage over Qt Quick/QML in terms of APIs and features.

In the next chapter, we're going to make our Qt applications redistributable and deploy them on other devices.

9
Deploying Applications on Other Devices

After development, it's time to distribute your application. We'll use an example application, `Internationalization`, from the previous chapter to demonstrate how to spread your Qt application to Windows, Linux, and Android. The following topics will be covered in this chapter:

- Releasing Qt applications on Windows
- Creating an installer
- Packaging Qt applications on Linux
- Deploying Qt applications on Android

Releasing Qt applications on Windows

After the development stage, you can build your application using `release` as the build configuration. In the `release` configuration, your compiler will optimize the code and won't produce debug symbols, which in turn reduces the size. Please ensure that the project is in the `release` configuration.

Before we jump into the packaging procedure, I'd like to talk about the difference between static and dynamic linking. You have probably been using dynamic linking of Qt libraries throughout this book. This can be confirmed if you download the **Community Edition** from the Qt website.

So, what does dynamic linking mean? Well, it means that when an executable file gets executed, the operating system will load and link the necessary shared libraries at runtime. In other words, you'll see a lot of .dll files on Windows and .so files on the Unix platforms. This technique allows developers to update these shared libraries and the executable separately, which means that you don't need to rebuild the executable file if you change shared libraries, so long as their ABIs are compatible. Although this method is more flexible, developers are warned to take care to avoid **DLL Hell**.

The most commonly used solution to DLL Hell on Windows is to choose static linking instead. By contrast, static linking will resolve all the function calls and variables at compile time and copy them into the target to produce a standalone executable. The advantages are obvious. Firstly, you don't need to ship all necessary and shared libraries. There won't be DLL Hell in this situation. On Windows, static libraries may get .lib or .a as extensions depending on the compiler you use, whereas they usually get .a on the Unix platforms.

To make a clear comparison, a table is made for you to see the differences between the dynamic and static linking:

	Dynamic Linking	**Static Linking**
Library types	Shared libraries	Static libraries
Executable size	Considerably smaller	Greater than dynamically linked
Library updates	Only libraries themselves	Executable file needs to be rebuilt
Incompatible libraries	Need to take care to avoid this	Won't happen

However, if the shared libraries shipped with dynamically linked executable files are counted as part of the package, the dynamic style package will be larger than the statically linked standalone executable files.

Now, back to the topic! Since there is no standard Qt runtime library installer for Windows, the best routine is to produce a statically linked target because the package to be released will be smaller, and the executable is immune to DLL Hell.

However, as mentioned previously, the Qt libraries you downloaded can only be used for dynamic linking applications because they are shared libraries. It is viable to compile Qt as static libraries. However, before you proceed, you need to know the licenses of Qt.

Currently, in addition to the Qt Open Source License, there is also the Qt Commercial License. For open source licenses, most of the Qt libraries are licensed under **The GNU Lesser General Public License (LPGL)**. In this case, if you build your application statically linked with the Qt libraries, your application is subject to provide users the source code of your application under LGPL. Your application may stay proprietary and closed source if it's dynamically linked with the Qt libraries. In other words, if you want to link an application statically and keep it proprietary, you have to purchase the Qt commercial license. For details about Qt licensing, refer to `http://www.qt.io/licensing/`.

If you decide to use static linking, you might have to compile the Qt libraries statically before building your application. In this case, the executable target is the only thing that needs to be packaged and released. Don't forget the QM files if your application has multi-language support, as mentioned previously.

On the other hand, if you want to go the dynamic way, it'd need some extra effort. Firstly, there are some core DLLs that have to exist and the list is different depending on the compiler. The following table includes both MSVC and MinGW/GCC scenarios:

MSVC 2013	**MinGW/GCC**
`msvcp120.dll`	`libgcc_s_dw2-1.dll`
`msvcr120.dll`	`libstdc++-6.dll`
	`libwinpthread-1.dll`

There are common DLLs that need to be included, such as `icudt53.dll`, `icuin53.dll`, and `icuuc53.dll`. You can find these files in the Qt libraries directory. Take MinGW/GCC as an example; they're located in `QT_DIR\5.4\mingw491_32\bin` where `QT_DIR` is the Qt installation path, such as `D:\Qt`. Note that the later versions of Qt may have slightly different filenames.

Besides, there is no need to ship `msvcp120.dll` and `msvcr120.dll` if the target users have installed **Visual C++ Redistributable Packages** for Visual Studio 2013, which can be downloaded from `http://www.microsoft.com/en-ie/download/details.aspx?id=40784`.

After this, you may want to check other DLLs you'll need by looking into the project file. Take the `Internationalization` project as an example. Its project file, `Internationalization.pro`, gives us a clue. There are two lines related to the QT configuration, shown as follows:

```
QT       += core gui

greaterThan(QT_MAJOR_VERSION, 4): QT += widgets
```

The `QT` variable includes the `core gui` widgets. In fact, all the Qt applications will include `core` at least, while others are dependent. In this case, we have to ship `Qt5Core.dll`, `Qt5Gui.dll`, and `Qt5Widgets.dll` along with the executable target.

Now, build the `Internationalization` project with MinGW/GCC. The executable target, `Internationalization.exe`, should be located inside the `release` folder of the build directory, which can be read from the **Projects** mode. Next, we create a new folder named `package` and copy the executable file there. Then, we copy the needed DLLs to `package` as well. Now, this folder should have all the necessary DLLs as shown here:

Name	Date modified	Type	Size
icudt53.dll	16/10/2014 11:34	Application extens...	21,061 KB
icuin53.dll	16/10/2014 11:34	Application extens...	3,671 KB
icuuc53.dll	16/10/2014 11:33	Application extens...	2,045 KB
Internationalization.exe	24/12/2014 22:43	Application	30 KB
libgcc_s_dw2-1.dll	23/10/2014 11:27	Application extens...	118 KB
libstdc++-6.dll	23/10/2014 11:27	Application extens...	1,003 KB
libwinpthread-1.dll	23/10/2014 11:27	Application extens...	48 KB
Qt5Core.dll	14/12/2014 22:41	Application extens...	4,720 KB
Qt5Gui.dll	05/12/2014 18:47	Application extens...	5,090 KB
Qt5Widgets.dll	14/12/2014 22:41	Application extens...	6,355 KB

In most cases, if a required library is missing, the application won't run while the operating system will prompt the missing library name. For instance, if `Qt5Widgets.dll` is missing, the following system error dialog will show up when you try to run `Internationalizationi.exe`:

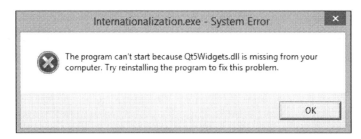

Basically, the routine is to copy the missing libraries to the same folder that the application is in. Besides, you can use some tools such as `Dependency Walker` to get the library dependencies.

Please don't use DLLs from the `Qt Editor` folder. This version is often different from Qt Libraries you've used. In addition to these libraries, you may have to include all the resources that your application is going to use. For example, the QM files used for translation, that is, to copy the `Internationalization_de.qm` file in order to load the German translation.

The file list is as follows:

- `icudt53.dll`
- `icuin53.dll`
- `icuuc53.dll`
- `Internationalization.exe`
- `Internationalization_de.qm`
- `libgcc_s_dw2-1.dll`
- `libstdc++-6.dll`
- `libwinpthread-1.dll`
- `Qt5Core.dll`
- `Qt5Gui.dll`
- `Qt5Widgets.dll`

Don't forget, this is the case for MinGW/GCC in Qt 5.4.0, while different versions and compilers might have a slightly different list, as we discussed before.

After this first-time preparation, to some extent this list is fixed. You only need to change the executable target and the QM file if it's changed. An easy way to do this is to compress all of them in `tarball`.

Creating an installer

Although it's quick to use an archive file to distribute your application, it seems more professional if you provide users with an installer. Qt offers **Qt Installer Framework** whose latest open source version, 1.5.0 for now, can be obtained from http://download.qt.io/official_releases/qt-installer-framework/1.5.0/.

For the sake of convenience, let's create a folder named `dist` under the Qt Installer Framework installation path, `D:\Qt\QtIFW-1.5.0`. This folder is used to store all the application projects that need to be packaged.

Then, create a folder named `internationalization` under `dist`. Inside `internationalization`, create two folders, `config` and `packages`.

The name of the directory inside the `packages` directory acts as a domain-like, or say Java-style, identifier. In this example, we have two packages, one is the application while the other one is a translation. Therefore, it adds to the two folders in the packages directory, `com.demo.internationalization`, and `com.demo.internationalization.translation`, respectively. There will be `meta` and `data` directories present inside each of them, so the overall directory structure is sketched as follows:

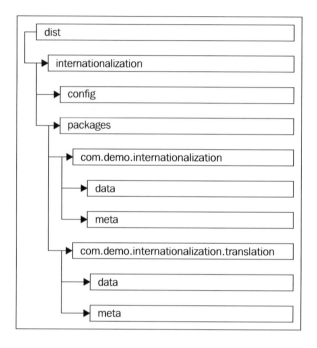

Let's edit the global configuration file, `config.xml`, which is first inside the `config` directory. You need to create one file named `config.xml`.

Always remember not to use the Windows built-in Notepad to edit this file, or in fact any file. You may either use Qt Creator or other advanced editors, such as Notepad++, to edit it. This is simply because Notepad lacks of a lot of features as a code editor.

In this example, the `config.xml` file's content is pasted here:

```xml
<?xml version="1.0" encoding="UTF-8"?>
<Installer>
  <Name>Internationalization</Name>
  <Version>1.0.0</Version>
  <Title>Internationalization Installer</Title>
  <Publisher>Packt</Publisher>
  <TargetDir>@homeDir@/Internationalization</TargetDir>
  <AdminTargetDir>@rootDir@/Internationalization</AdminTargetDir>
</Installer>
```

For a minimum `config.xml` file, the elements `<Name>` and `<Version>` must exist in `<Installer>`. All other elements are optional, but you should specify them if there is a need. Meanwhile, `<TargetDir>` and `<AdminTargetDir>` may be a bit confusing. They both specify the default installation path, where `<AdminTargetDir>` is to specify the installation path when it gained administrative rights. The other elements are pretty much self-explanatory. There are other elements that you can set to customize the installer. For more details, refer to http://doc.qt.io/ qtinstallerframework/ifw-globalconfig.html.

Let's navigate into the `meta` folder inside `com.demo.internationalization`. This directory contains the files that specify the settings for deployment and installation. All the files in this directory, except for licenses, won't be extracted by the installer, and neither will they be installed. There must be at least a package information file, such as `package.xml`. The following example, `package.xml`, in `com.demo. internationalization/meta` is shown here:

```xml
<?xml version="1.0" encoding="UTF-8"?>
<Package>
  <DisplayName>Core Application</DisplayName>
  <Description>Essential part of
    Internationalization</Description>
  <Version>1.0.0</Version>
  <ReleaseDate>2014-12-27</ReleaseDate>
  <Name>com.demo.internationalization</Name>
  <Licenses>
    <License name="License Agreement" file="license.txt" />
  </Licenses>
  <Default>true</Default>
  <ForcedInstallation>true</ForcedInstallation>
</Package>
```

The `<Default>` element specifies whether this package should be selected by default. At the same time, we set `<ForcedInstallation>` to `true`, indicating that the end users can't deselect this package. While the `<Licenses>` element can have multiple children `<License>`, in this case we only have one. We have to provide the `license.txt` file, whose content is just a single line demonstration, as shown here:

```
This is the content of license.txt.
```

The following `package.xml` file, which is located in `com.demo.internationalization.translation/meta`, has fewer lines:

```xml
<?xml version="1.0" encoding="UTF-8"?>
<Package>
  <DisplayName>German Translation</DisplayName>
  <Description>German translation file</Description>
  <Version>1.0.0</Version>
  <ReleaseDate>2014-12-27</ReleaseDate>
  <Name>com.demo.internationalization.translation</Name>
  <Default>false</Default>
</Package>
```

The difference between `<DisplayName>` and `<Description>` is demonstrated by the following screenshot:

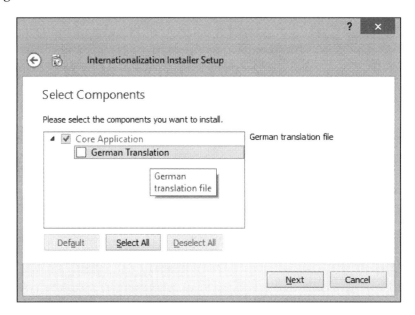

The `<Description>` element is the text that displays on the right-hand side when the package gets selected. It's also the text that pops up as the tooltip when the mouse hovers over the entry. You can also see the relationship between these two packages. As the name `com.demo.internationalization.translation` suggests, it is a subpackage of `com.demo.internationalization`.

The licenses will be displayed after this step and are shown in the following screenshot. If you set multiple licenses, the dialog will have a panel to view those licenses separately, similar to the one you see when you install Qt itself.

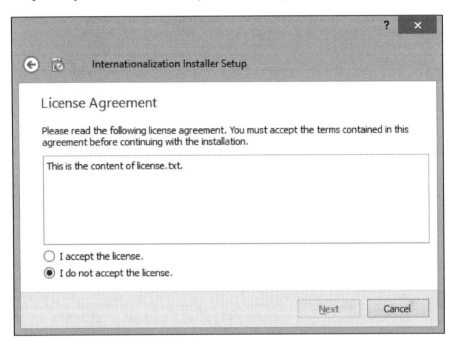

For more settings in the `package.xml` file, refer to `http://doc.qt.io/ qtinstallerframework/ifw-component-description.html#package- information-file-syntax`.

By contrast, the `data` directories store all the files that need to be installed. In this example, we keep all files prepared previously in the `data` folder of `com.demo.internationalization`, except for the QM file. The QM file, `Internationalization_de.qm`, is kept in the `data` folder inside `com.demo. internationalization.translation`.

After all the initial preparation, we come to the final step to generate the installer application of this project. Depending on your operating system, open **Command Prompt** or **Terminal**, changing the current directory to dist/internationalization. In this case, it's D:\Qt\QtIFW-1.5.0\dist\ internationalization. Then, execute the following command to generate the internationalization_installer.exe installer file:

..\..\bin\binarycreator.exe -c config\config.xml -p packages
internationalization_installer.exe

> On Unix platforms, including Linux and Mac OS X, you'll have to use a slash (/) instead of anti-slash (\), and drop the .exe suffix, which makes the command slightly different, as shown here:
>
> ```
> ../../bin/binarycreator -c config/config.xml -p
> packages internationalization_installer
> ```

You need to wait for a while because the binarycreator tool will package files in the data directories into the 7zip archives, which is a time consuming process. After this, you should expect to see internationalization_installer.exe (or without .exe) in the current directory.

The installer is much more convenient, especially for a big application project that has several optional packages. Besides, it'll register and let the end users uninstall through **Control Panel**.

Packaging Qt applications on Linux

Things are more complicated on Linux than on Windows. There are two popular package formats: **RPM Package Manager** (RPM) and **Debian Binary Package** (DEB). RPM was originally developed for **Red Hat Linux** and it's the baseline package format of **Linux Standard Base**. It's mainly used on **Fedora**, **OpenSUSE**, **Red Hat Enterprise Linux**, and its derivatives; while the latter is famous for being used in **Debian** and its well-known and popular derivative, **Ubuntu**.

In addition to these formats, there are other Linux distributions using different package formats, such as **Arch Linux** and **Gentoo**. It will take extra time to package your applications for different Linux distributions.

However, it won't be too time consuming, especially for open-source applications. If your application is open source, you can refer to the documentation to write a formatted script to compile and package your application. For details on creating an RPM package, refer to `https://fedoraproject.org/wiki/How_to_create_an_RPM_package`, whereas for DEB packaging, refer to `https://www.debian.org/doc/manuals/maint-guide/index.en.html`. There is an example later that demonstrates how to package DEB.

Although it's feasible to pack proprietary applications, such as the RPM and DEB packages, they won't get into the official repository. In this case, you may want to set up a repository on your server or just release the packages via a file host.

Alternatively, you can archive your applications, similar to what we do on Windows, and write a shell script for installation and uninstallation. In this way, you can use one tarball or Qt Installer Framework to cook an installer for various distributions. But, don't ever forget to address the dependencies appropriately. The incompatible shared library issue is even worse on Linux, because almost all the libraries and applications are linked dynamically. The worst part is the incompatibility between different distributions, since they may use different library versions. Therefore, either take care of these pitfalls, or go the static linking way.

As we mentioned previously, statically linked software must be open source unless you have purchased the Qt commercial license. This dilemma makes the statically linked open source application pointless. This is not only because dynamic linking is the standard way, but also because statically linked Qt applications won't be able to use the system theme and can't benefit from system upgrades, which is not okay when security updates are involved. Anyway, you can compile your application using static linking if your application is proprietary and you get a commercial license. In this case, just like static linking on Windows, you only need to release the target executable files with the necessary resources, such as icons and translations. It's noteworthy that even if you build statically linked Qt applications, it's still impossible to run them on any Linux distributions.

Therefore, the recommended way is to install several mainstream Linux distributions on virtual machines, and then use these virtual machines to package your dynamically linked application as their own package formats. The binary package doesn't contain source code, and it's also a common practice to strip the symbols from the binary package. In this way, your source code for proprietary software won't be leaked through these packages.

We still use `Internationalization` as an example here. Let's see how to create a DEB package. The following operations were tested on the latest **Debian Wheezy**; later versions or different Linux distributions might be slightly different.

Before we package the application, we have to edit the project file,
`Internationalization.pro`, to make it installable as follows:

```
QT          += core gui

greaterThan(QT_MAJOR_VERSION, 4): QT += widgets

TARGET = Internationalization
TEMPLATE = app


SOURCES += main.cpp \
           mainwindow.cpp

HEADERS  += mainwindow.h

FORMS    += mainwindow.ui

TRANSLATIONS = Internationalization_de.ts

unix: {
    target.path  = /opt/internationalization_demo
    qmfile.path  = $$target.path
    qmfile.files = Internationalization_de.qm

    INSTALLS += target \
                qmfile
}
```

There is a concept in qmake called **install set**. Each install set has three members:
`path`, `files`, and `extra`. The `path` member defines the destination location, while
`files` tells qmake what files should be copied. You can specify some commands that
need to be executed before other instructions in `extra`.

TARGET is a bit special. Firstly, it's the target executable (or library), while on the
other hand, it also implies `target.files`. Therefore, we only need to specify the
path of `target`. We also use the same path for `qmfile`, which includes the QM file.
Don't forget to use a double dollar sign, `$$`, to use a variable. Lastly, we set the
INSTALLS variable, which defines what is to be installed when `make install` is
called. The `unix` brackets are used to limit the lines only read by qmake on the
Unix platforms.

Now, we can get into the DEB packaging part by performing the following steps:

1. Change your working directory (current directory) to the root of the project, that is, `~/Internationalization`.

2. Create a new folder named `debian`.

3. Create the four required files in the `debian` folder: `control`, `copyright`, `changelog`, and `rules`, respectively. Then, create an optional `compat` file in the `debian` folder as well.

The `control` file defines the most basic yet most critical things. This file is all about the source package and the binary package(s). The `control` file of our example is pasted here:

```
Source: internationalization
Section: misc
Priority: extra
Maintainer: Symeon Huang <hzwhuang@gmail.com>
Build-Depends: debhelper (>=9),
               qt5-qmake,
               qtbase5-dev,
               qtbase5-private-dev
Standards-Version: 3.9.6

Package: internationalization
Architecture: any
Depends: ${shlibs:Depends}, ${misc:Depends}
Description: An example of Qt5 Blueprints
```

The first paragraph is to control information for a source, whereas each of the following sets describe a binary package that the source tree builds. In other words, one source package may build several binary packages. In this case, we build only one binary package whose name is the same as `Source` and `internationalization`.

In the `Source` paragraph, `Source` and `Maintainer` are mandatory while `Section`, `Priority`, and `Standards-Version` are recommended. `Source` identifies the source package name, which can't include uppercase letters. Meanwhile, `Maintainer` contains the maintainer package's name and the e-mail address in the RFC822 format. The `Section` field specifies an application area in which the package has been classified. `Priority` is a self-explanatory field, indicating how important this package is. Lastly, `Standards-Version` describes the most recent version of the standards with which the package complies. In most cases, you should use the latest standard version, 3.9.6 for now. There are other fields that may be useful but optional. For more details, refer to https://www.debian.org/doc/debian-policy/ch-controlfields.html.

You can specify certain packages needed for building in `Build-Depends`, similar to `qt5-qmake` and `qtbase5-dev` in our example. They're only defined for building processes and won't be included in the dependencies of binary packages.

The binary paragraphs are similar to the source except that there is no `Maintainer`, but `Architecture` and `Description` are mandatory now. For binary packages, `Architecture` can be any particular architecture or simply `any` or `all`. Specifying `any` indicates that the source package isn't dependent on any particular architecture and hence can be built on any architecture. In contrast to this, `all` means that the source package will produce only architecture-independent packages, such as documentations and scripts.

In `Depends` of the binary paragraph, we put `${shlibs:Depends}`, `${misc:Depends}` instead of particular packages. The `${shlibs:Depends}` line can be used to let `dpkg-shlibdeps` generate shared library dependencies automatically. On the other hand, according to `debhepler`, you're encouraged to put `${misc:Depends}` in the field to supplement `${shlibs:Depends}`. In this way, we don't need to specify the dependencies manually, which is a relief for packagers.

The second required file, `copyright`, is to describe the licenses of the source as well as the DEB packages. In the `copyright` file, the format field is required while the others are optional. For more details about the formats of copyright, refer to `https://www.debian.org/doc/packaging-manuals/copyright-format/1.0/`. The `copyright` file in this example is shown as follows:

```
Format: http://www.debian.org/doc/packaging-manuals/copyright-
   format/1.0/
Upstream-Contact: Symeon Huang <hzwhuang@gmail.com>

File: *
Copyright: 2014, 2015 Symeon Huang
License: Packt

License: Packt
  This package is released under Packt license.
```

The first paragraph is called **Header paragraph**, which is needed once and only once. The `Format` line is the only mandatory field in this paragraph, and in most cases, this line is the same. The syntax of the `Upstream-Contact` field is the same as `Maintainer` in the `control` file.

The second paragraph in this file is **Files paragraph**, which is mandatory and repeatable. In these paragraphs, File, Copyright, and License are required. We use an asterisk sign (*) indicating that this paragraph applies to all files. The Copyright field may contain the original statement copied from files or a shortened text. The License field in a Files paragraph describes the licensing terms for the files defined by File.

Following the Files paragraph, the **Stand-alone license paragraph** is optional and repeatable. We have to provide the full license text if the license is not provided by Debian. Generally speaking, only commonly-seen open-source licenses are provided. The first line must be a single license short name, which is then followed by a license text. For a license text, there must be a two space indentation in each line's head.

Don't be misled by the changelog filename. This file also has a special format and is used by dpkg to obtain the version number, revision, distribution, and urgency of your package. It's a good practice to document all the changes you have made in this file. However, you can just list the most important ones if you have a version control system. The changelog file in our example has the following contents:

```
internationalization (1.0.0-1) unstable; urgency=low

  * Initial release

 -- Symeon Huang <hzwhuang@gmail.com>  Mon, 29 Dec 2014 18:45:31
    +0000
```

The first line is the package name, version, distribution, and urgency. The name must match the source package name. In this example, internationalization is the name, 1.0.0-1 is the version, unstable stands for the distribution, and urgency is low. Then, use an empty line to separate the first line and log entries. In the log entries, all the changes that you want to document should be listed. For each entry, there are two spaces and an asterisk sign (*) in the header. The last part of a paragraph is a maintainer line that begins with a space. For more details about this file and its format, refer to https://www.debian.org/doc/debian-policy/ch-source.html#s-dpkgchangelog.

Now, we need to take a look at what `dpkg-buildpackage` will do to create the package. This process is controlled by the `rules` file; the example is pasted here:

```
#!/usr/bin/make -f

export QT_SELECT := qt5

%:
   dh $@

override_dh_auto_configure:
   qmake
```

This file, similar to `Makefile`, consists of several rules. Also, each rule begins with its target declaration, while the recipes are the following lines beginning with the TAB code (not four spaces). We explicitly set Qt 5 as the Qt version, which can avoid some issues when Qt 5 coexists with Qt 4. The percentage sign (`%`) is a special target and means any targets, which just calls the `dh` program with the target name, while `dh` is just a wrapper script, which runs appropriate programs depending on its argument, the real target.

The rest of the lines are customizations for the `dh` command. For instance, `dh_auto_configure` will call `./configure` by default. In our case, we use `qmake` to generate `Makefile` instead of a configure script. Therefore, we override `dh_auto_configure` by adding the `override_dh_auto_configure` target with `qmake` as the recipe.

Although the `compat` file is optional, you'll get bombarded with warnings if you don't specify it. Currently, you should set its content to `9`, which can be done by the following single-line command:

echo 9 > debian/compat

We can generate the binary DEB package now. The `-uc` argument stands for uncheck while `-us` stands for unsign. If you have a PKG key, you may need to sign the package so that users can trust the packages you've released. We don't need source packages, so the last argument, `-b`, indicates that only the binary packages will be built.

dpkg-buildpackage -uc -us -b

The automatically detected dependencies can be viewed in the `debian/` file, `internationalization.substvars`. This file's contents are pasted here:

```
shlibs:Depends=libc6 (>= 2.13-28), libc6 (>= 2.4), libgcc1 (>=
  1:4.4.0), libqt5core5a (>= 5.0.2), libqt5gui5 (>= 5.0.2),
    libqt5widgets5 (>= 5.0.2), libstdc++6 (>= 4.3.0)
misc:Depends=
```

As we discussed earlier, the dependencies are generated by `shlibs` and `misc`. The biggest advantage is that these generated version numbers tend to be the smallest, which means the maximum backwards compatibility. As you can see, our `Internationalization` example can run on Qt 5.0.2.

If everything goes well, you'd expect a DEB file in an upper-level directory. However, you can only build the current architecture's binary package, `amd64`. If you want to build for `i386` natively, you need to install a 32-bit x86 Debian. For cross-compilation, refer to `https://wiki.debian.org/CrossBuildPackagingGuidelines` and `https://wiki.ubuntu.com/CrossBuilding`.

Installing a local DEB file is easily done with the following single-line command:

```
sudo dpkg -i internationalization_1.0.0-1_amd64.deb
```

After installation, we can run our application by running `/opt/internationalization_demo/Internationalization`. It should run as expected and behave exactly the same as on Windows, as shown in the following screenshot:

Deploying Qt applications on Android

The `internationalization` application requires a QM file to be loaded correctly. On Windows and Linux, we choose to install them alongside the target executable. However, this is not always a good approach, especially on Android. The path is more complicated than the desktop operating systems. Besides, we're building a Qt application instead of the Java application. Localization is definitely different from a plain Java application, as stated in the Android documentation. Hence, we're going to bundle all the resources into the `qrc` file, which will be built into the binary target:

1. Add a new file to project by right-clicking on the project, and then select **Add New...**.

2. Navigate to **Qt | Qt Resource File** in the **New File** dialog.

3. Name it `res` and click on **OK**; Qt Creator will redirect you to edit `res.qrc`.

4. Navigate to **Add | Add Prefix** and change **Prefix** to `/`.

5. Navigate to **Add | Add Files** and select the.`Internationalization_de.qm` file in the dialog.

Now, we need to edit `mainwindow.cpp` to make it load the translation file from `Resources`. We only need to change the constructor of `MainWindow` where we load the translation, as shown here:

```
MainWindow::MainWindow(QWidget *parent) :
  QMainWindow(parent),
  ui(new Ui::MainWindow)
{
  ui->setupUi(this);

  deTranslator = new QTranslator(this);
  deTranslator->load(QLocale::German, "Internationalization", "_",
    ":/");
  deLoaded = false;

  connect(ui->openButton, &QPushButton::clicked, this,
    &MainWindow::onOpenButtonClicked);
  connect(ui->loadButton, &QPushButton::clicked, this,
    &MainWindow::onLoadButtonClicked);
}
```

The preceding code is to specify the directory for the `QTranslator::load` function. As we mentioned in the previous chapter, `:/` indicates that it's a `qrc` path. Don't add a `qrc` prefix unless it's a `QUrl` object.

We can remove the `qmfile` install set from the project file now, because we've already bundled the QM file. In other words, after this change, you don't need to ship the QM file on Windows or Linux anymore. Edit the project file, `Internationalization.pro`, as shown in the following code:

```
QT        += core gui

greaterThan(QT_MAJOR_VERSION, 4): QT += widgets

TARGET = Internationalization
TEMPLATE = app


SOURCES += main.cpp \
           mainwindow.cpp

HEADERS   += mainwindow.h
```

```
FORMS     += mainwindow.ui

TRANSLATIONS = Internationalization_de.ts

unix: {
    target.path  = /opt/internationalization_demo

    INSTALLS += target
}

RESOURCES += \
    res.qrc
```

Now, switch to **Projects** mode and add the **Android** kit. Don't forget to switch the build to `release`. In **Projects** mode, you can modify how Qt Creator should build the Android APK package. There is an entry in **Build Steps** called **Build Android APK**, as shown in the following screenshot:

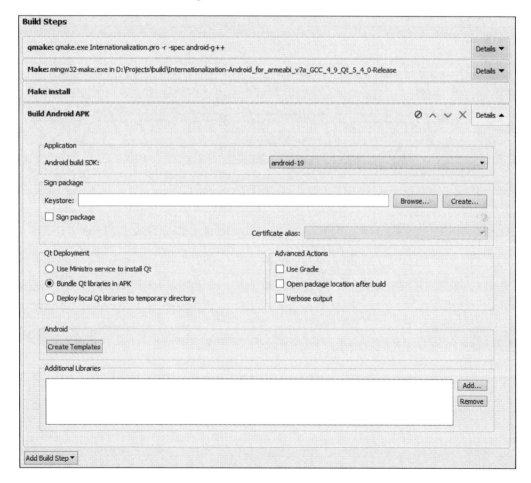

Here, you can specify the Android API level and your certificate. By default, **Qt Deployment** is set to **Bundle Qt libraries in APK**, which creates a redistributable APK file. Let's click on the **Create Templates** button to generate a manifest file, AndroidManifest.xml. Normally, you just click on the **Finish** button on the pop-up dialog, and then Qt Creator will redirect you back to the **Edit** mode with AndroidManifest.xml open in the editing area, as shown here:

Package	
Package name:	com.demo.internationalization
Version code:	1
Version name:	1.0
Minimum required SDK:	API 14: Android 4.0, 4.0.1, 4.0.2
Target SDK:	API 19: Android 4.4
Application	
Application name:	-- %%INSERT_APP_NAME%% --
Run:	-- %%INSERT_APP_LIB_NAME%% --
Application icon:	
Permissions	
☑ Include default permissions for Qt modules.	
☑ Include default features for Qt modules.	

Let's make a few changes to this manifest file by performing the following steps:

1. Change **Package name** to com.demo.internationalization.
2. Change **Minimum required SDK** to API 14: Android 4.0, 4.0.1, 4.0.2.
3. Change **Target SDK** to API 19: Android 4.4.
4. Save the changes.

Different API levels have an impact on compatibility and the UI; you have to decide the levels carefully. In this case, we require at least Android 4.0 to run this application, which we're going to it for Android 4.4. Generally speaking, the higher the API level, the better the overall performance is. The Internationalization.pro project file is automatically changed as well.

```
QT          += core gui

greaterThan(QT_MAJOR_VERSION, 4): QT += widgets

TARGET = Internationalization
TEMPLATE = app


SOURCES += main.cpp \
           mainwindow.cpp

HEADERS  += mainwindow.h

FORMS    += mainwindow.ui

TRANSLATIONS = Internationalization_de.ts

unix: {
    target.path  = /opt/internationalization_demo

    INSTALLS += target
}

RESOURCES += \
res.qrc

DISTFILES += \
    android/gradle/wrapper/gradle-wrapper.jar \
    android/AndroidManifest.xml \
    android/res/values/libs.xml \
    android/build.gradle \
    android/gradle/wrapper/gradle-wrapper.properties \
    android/gradlew \
    android/gradlew.bat


ANDROID_PACKAGE_SOURCE_DIR = $$PWD/android
```

Now, build a `release` build. The APK file is created in `android-build/bin` inside the project build directory. The APK filename is `QtApp-release.apk` or `QtApp-debug.apk` if you don't set your certificate. If you're going to submit your application to Google Play or any other Android markets, you have to set your certificate and upload `QtApp-release.apk` instead of `QtApp-debug.apk`. Meanwhile, `QtApp-debug.apk` can be used on your own devices to test the functionality of your application.

The screenshot of `Internationalization` running on HTC One is shown as follows:

As you can see, the German translation is loaded as expected, while the pop-up dialog has a native look and feel.

Summary

In this chapter, we compared the advantages and disadvantages of static and dynamic linking. Later on, we used an example application, showing you how to create an installer on Windows and how to package it as a DEB package on Debian Linux. Last but not least, we also learned how to create a redistributable APK file for Android. The slogan, *code less, create more, deploy everywhere* is now fulfilled.

In the next chapter, which is also the last chapter of this book, in addition to how to debug applications, we're also going to look at some common issues and solutions to them.

10
Don't Panic When You Encounter These Issues

During application development, you may get stuck with some issues. Qt is amazing, as always, since Qt Creator has an excellent **Debug** mode that can save you time when debugging. You'll learn how to debug either Qt/C++ or Qt Quick/QML applications. The following topics will be covered in this chapter:

- Commonly encountered issues
- Debugging Qt applications
- Debugging Qt Quick applications
- Useful resources

Commonly encountered issues

Errors, or more appropriately, unexpected results, are definitely unavoidable during application development. Besides, there could also be compiler errors, or even application crashes. Please don't panic when you encounter these kinds of issues. To ease your pain and help you locate the problem, we have collected some commonly encountered and reproducible unexpected results and categorized them, as shown in the next sections.

C++ syntax mistakes

For programming beginners, or developers who are not familiar with C and C++, the syntax of C++ is not easy to remember. If there are any syntax mistakes, the compiler will abort with error messages. In fact, the editor will display tildes below problematic statements, as shown here:

```
main.cpp*                              ×    main(int, char *[]): int
1    #include "mainwindow.h"
2    #include <QApplication>
3
4  ◢ int main(int argc, char *argv[])
5    {
6        QApplication a(argc, argv);
7|       MainWindow w
8        w.show();
9
10       return a.exec();
11   }
12
```

Among all C++ syntax mistakes, the most common one is a missing semicolon (;). C++ needs a semicolon to mark the end of a statement. Therefore, line 7 and line 8 are equivalent to the following line:

```
MainWindow w w.show();
```

This, in C++, is obviously written incorrectly. Not only will the editor highlight the error, the compiler will also give you a thorough error message. In this case, it'll display the following message:

```
C:\Users\Symeon\OneDrive\Book_Dev\46150S\46150S_07\project\Weather_
Demo\main.cpp:8: error: C2146: syntax error : missing ';' before
identifier 'w'
```

As you can tell, the compiler won't tell you that you should add a semicolon at the end of line 7. Instead, it reads missing; before the w identifier, which is in line 8. Anyway, in most cases the C++ syntax errors can be detected by the compiler, while most of them will first be detected by the editor. Thanks to the highlighting feature of Qt Creator, these types of mistakes should be avoided effectively.

It's recommended as a good habit that you add a semicolon before you press *Enter*. This is because in some cases the syntax may seem correct for compilers and Qt Creator, but it's definitely wrongly coded and will cause unexpected behavior.

Pointer and memory

Anyone familiar with C and its wild pointers understands how easy it is to make a mistake regarding memory management. As we mentioned before, Qt has a superior memory management mechanism, which will release its child objects once the parent is deleted. This, unfortunately, may lead to a crash if the developer explicitly uses `delete` to release a child object.

The primary reason behind this is that `delete` is not a thread-safe operation. It may cause a double delete, resulting in a segment fault. Therefore, to release memory in a thread-safe way, we use the `deleteLater()` function defined in the `QObject` class, which means that this method is available for all classes inherited from `QObject`. As stated in the documentation, `deleteLater()` will schedule the object for deletion but the deletion won't happen immediately.

 It's completely safe to call `deleteLater()` multiple times. Once the first deferred deletion is completed, any pending deletions are removed from the event queue. There won't be any double deletes.

There is another class dealing with memory management in Qt, `QObjectCleanupHandler`. This class watches the lifetime of multiple QObjects. You can treat it as a simple Qt garbage collector. For instance, there are a lot of `QTcpSocket` objects that need to be watched and deleted properly. These kinds of cases are not uncommon, especially for networking programs. An easy trick is to add all these objects to `QObjectCleanupHandler`. The following piece of code is a simple demonstration that adds `QObject` to `QObjectCleanupHandler ch`:

```
QTcpSocket *t = new QTcpSocket(this);
QObjectCleanupHandler ch;
ch.add(t);
```

Adding the `t` object to `ch` won't change the parent object of `t` from this to `&ch`. `QObjectCleanupHandler` is more like `QList` in this way. If `t` is deleted somewhere else, it'll get removed from the list of `ch` automatically. If there is no object left, the `isEmpty()` function will return `true`. All objects in `QObjectCleanupHandler` will be deleted when it's destroyed. You can also explicitly call `clear()` to delete all objects in `QObjectCleanupHandler` manually.

Incompatible shared libraries

This type of errors are the so-called DLL Hell, which we discussed in the previous chapter. It results from incompatible shared libraries, which may lead to strange behavior or crashes.

In most cases, Qt libraries are backwards compatible, which means that you may replace all DLLs with newer ones and not need to recompile executables. Some certain modules or APIs may be deprecated and be deleted from a later version of Qt. For example, the QGLWidget class is replaced by a newly introduced QOpenGLWidget class in Qt 5.4. QGLWidget is still provided for now though.

In the reverse direction, things are getting pretty bad. If your application calls an API that is introduced since, for example, Qt 5.4, the application definitely will malfunction with an older version of Qt, such as Qt 5.2.

The following is a simple program that makes use of QSysInfo, which is introduced in Qt 5.4. The main.cpp file of this simple incompat_demo project is shown here:

```cpp
#include <QDebug>
#include <QSysInfo>
#include <QCoreApplication>

int main(int argc, char *argv[])
{
    QCoreApplication a(argc, argv);

    qDebug() << "CPU:" << QSysInfo::currentCpuArchitecture();

    return a.exec();
}
```

QSysInfo::currentCpuArchitecture() returns the architecture of the CPU that the application is running on as a QString object. If the version of Qt is high enough (greater than or equal to 5.4), it'll run as expected, as shown in the following screenshot:

As you can see, it says we're running this application on a 64-bit x86 CPU machine. However, if we put the compiled executable with DLLs from Qt 5.2, it'll give an error as shown here and crash:

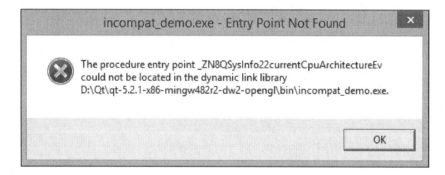

This situation is rare, of course. However, if this happens, you'll get an idea about what goes wrong. From the error dialog, we can see the error is because of the missing `QSysInfo::currentCpuArchitecture` line in the dynamic link library.

Another DLL Hell is more complex and may be ignored by beginners. All libraries must be built by the same compiler. You can't use the MSVC libraries with GCC, which holds true for other compilers, such as ICC and Clang. Different compiler versions might cause incompatibility as well. You probably don't want to use a library compiled by GCC 4.3 in your development environment where the GCC version is 4.9. However, libraries compiled by GCC 4.9.1 should be compatible with those compiled by GCC 4.9.2.

In addition to compilers, different architectures are often incompatible. For example, 64-bit libraries won't work on 32-bit platforms. Similarly, x86 libraries and binaries can't be used on the non-x86 devices, such as ARM and MIPS.

Doesn't run on Android!

Qt was ported to Android not too long ago. Hence, there is a possibility that it runs well on a desktop PC but not on Android. On one hand, Android hardware varies, not even speaking of thousands of customized ROMs. Therefore, it is reasonable that some Android devices may encounter compatibility issues. On the other hand, the Qt application running on Android is a native C++ application with a Java wrapper, while binary executables are naturally more vulnerable to compatibility issues than scripts.

Anyway, here's the recipe:

1. Try to run your application on another Android handset or virtual Android device.

2. If it still doesn't work, it can be a potential bug of Qt on Android. We'll talk about how to report a bug to Qt at the end of this chapter.

Debugging Qt applications

To debug any Qt application, you need to ensure that you have installed the debug symbols of the Qt libraries. On Windows, they are installed together with release version DLLs. Meanwhile, on Linux, you may need to install debug symbols by the distribution's package manager.

Some developers tend to use a function similar to `printf` to debug the application. Qt provides four global functions, which are shown in the following table, to print out debug, warnings, and error text:

Function	Usage
qDebug()	This function is used for writing custom debug output.
qWarning()	This function is used for reporting warnings and recoverable errors.
qCritical()	This function is used for writing critical error messages and reporting system errors.
qFatal()	This function is used for printing fatal error messages shortly before exiting.

Normally, you can just use a C-style method similar to `printf`.

```
qDebug("Hello %s", "World!");
```

However, in most cases, we'll include the `<QtDebug>` header file so that we can use the stream operator (`<<`) as a more convenient way.

```
qDebug() << "Hello World!"
```

The most powerful place of these functions is that they can output the contents of some complex classes', `QList` and `QMap`. It's noted that these complex data types can only be printed through a stream operator (`<<`).

Both `qDebug()` and `qWarning()` are debugging tools, which mean that they can be disabled at compile time by defining `QT_NO_DEBUG_OUTPUT` and `QT_NO_WARNING_OUTPUT`, respectively.

In addition to these functions, Qt also provides the `QObject::dumpObjectTree()` and `QObject::dumpObjectInfo()` functions which are often useful, especially when an application looks strange. `QObject::dumpObjectTree()` dumps information about signal connections, which is really useful if you think there may be a problem in signal slot connections. Meanwhile, the latter dumps a tree of children to the debug output. Don't forget to build the application in **Debug** mode, otherwise neither of them will print anything.

Apart from these useful debugging functions, Qt Creator has offered an intuitive way to debug your application. Ensure that you've installed Microsoft **Console debugger (CDB)** if you're using an MSVC compiler. In other cases, the GDB debugger is bundled in a MinGW version.

 CDB is now a part of **Windows Driver Kit (WDK)**; visit `http://msdn.microsoft.com/en-us/windows/hardware/hh852365` to download it. Don't forget to check Debugging Tools for Windows during the installation.

Consider `Fancy_Clock` from *Chapter 2, Building a Beautiful Cross-platform Clock*, as an example. In the `MainWindow::setColour()` function, move the cursor to line 97, which is `switch (i) {`. Then, navigate to **Debug | Toggle Breakpoint** or just press *F9* on the keyboard. This will add a breakpoint on line 97, which will add a breakpoint marker (a red pause icon in front of a line number) as shown here:

```
 92   void MainWindow::setColour()
 93   {
 94       QSettings sts;
 95       int i = sts.value("Colour").toInt();
 96       QPalette c;
 97       switch (i) {
 98       case 0://black
 99           c.setColor(QPalette::Foreground, Qt::black);
100           break;
101       case 1://white
102           c.setColor(QPalette::Foreground, Qt::white);
103           break;
104       case 2://green
105           c.setColor(QPalette::Foreground, Qt::green);
106           break;
107       case 3://red
108           c.setColor(QPalette::Foreground, Qt::red);
109           break;
110       }
111       ui->lcdNumber->setPalette(c);
112       this->update();
113   }
114
```

Now click on the **Start Debugging** button on the pane, which has a bug on it, or navigate to **Debug | Start Debugging | Start Debugging** on the menu bar, or press *F5* on the keyboard. This will recompile the application, if needed, and start it in **Debug** mode. At the same time, Qt Creator will automatically switch to **Debug** mode.

```
 95       int i = sts.value("Colour").toInt();
 96       QPalette c;
 97       switch (i) {
 98       case 0://black
 99           c.setColor(QPalette::Foreground, Qt::black);
100           break;
101       case 1://white
102           c.setColor(QPalette::Foreground, Qt::white);
103           break;
104       case 2://green
105           c.setColor(QPalette::Foreground, Qt::green);
106           break;
107       case 3://red
108           c.setColor(QPalette::Foreground, Qt::red);
109           break;
110       }
```

The application is interrupted because of the breakpoint we set. You can see a yellow arrow indicating which line the application is currently on, as shown in the preceding screenshot. By default, on the right pane, you can see **Locals and Expressions** where all the local variables along with their values and types are shown. To change the default settings, navigate to **Window | Views**, and then choose what to display or hide.

The panes in the **Debug** mode are marked in blue text in this screenshot:

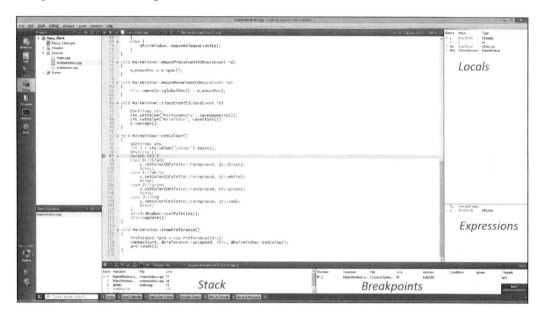

Briefly said, you can monitor the variables in **Locals** and expressions in **Expressions**. **Stack** displays the current stack and all breakpoints can be managed in the **Breakpoints** pane.

On the bottom pane, there are a series of buttons to control the debugging process. The first six buttons are **Continue**, **Stop Debugger**, **Step Over**, **Step Into**, **Step Out**, and **Restart the debugging session**, respectively. **Step Over** is to execute a line of code as a whole. **Step Into** will step into a function or a subfunction, while **Step Out** can leave the current function or subfunction.

Breakpoints plays a crucial role in debugging, as you can tell whether a breakpoint represents a position or set of positions in the code that interrupts the application from being debugged and grants you control. Once it is interrupted, you can examine the state of the program or continue the execution, either line-by-line or continuously. Qt Creator shows breakpoints in the **Breakpoints** view, which is located at the lower-right-hand side by default. You can add or delete breakpoints in the **Breakpoints** view. To add a breakpoint, right-click on the **Breakpoints** view and select **Add Breakpoint...**; there will be an **Add Breakpoint** dialog as shown here:

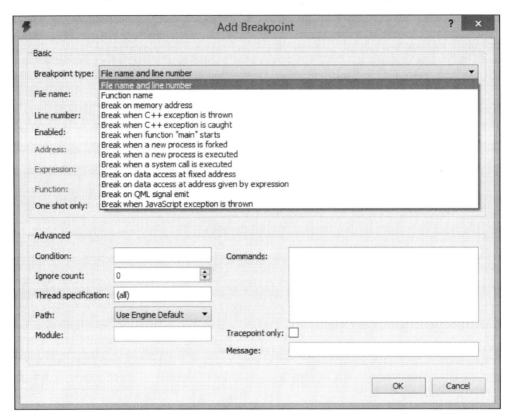

In the **Breakpoint type** field, select the location in the program code where you want the application to be interrupted. Other options are dependent on the selected type.

To move the breakpoint, simply drag the breakpoint marker and drop it on the destination. It's not an often needed function, though.

There're many ways to delete a breakpoint.

- By clicking on the breakpoint marker in the editor, moving the cursor to the corresponding line, and navigating to **Debug | Toggle Breakpoint**, or by pressing *F9*

- By right-clicking on the breakpoint in the **Breakpoints** view and selecting **Delete Breakpoint**

- By selecting the breakpoint in the **Breakpoints** view and pressing the *Delete* button on the keyboard

The most powerful place is the previously introduced **Locals and Expressions** view. Every time the program stops under the control of the debugger, it retrieves information and displays it in the **Locals and Expressions** view. The **Locals** pane shows function parameters and local variables. There is a comprehensive display of data belonging to Qt's basic objects. In this case, when the program is interrupted in `MainWindow::setColour()`, there is a pointer whose **Value** is `"MainWindow"`. Instead of just memory address of this pointer, it can show you all the data and children that belong to this object:

Name	Value	Type
▷ c	@0x28fc98	QPalette
i	3	int
▷ sts	@0x28fca0	QSettings
▲ this	"MainWindow"	MainWindow
▲ [QMainWindow]	"MainWindow"	QMainWindow
▷ [QWidget]	"MainWindow"	QWidget
▷ [children]	<3 items>	QObjectList
▷ [methods]	<5 items>	
▷ [parent]	@0x28fe24	QWidget
▷ [properties]	<more than 0 items>	
▷ [signals]	<2 items>	
▷ staticMetaObject	@0x9559958	QMetaObject
▲ [children]	<3 items>	QObjectList
▷ [0]	"_layout"	QMainWindowLayout
▷ [1]	"qt_rubberband"	QRubberBand
▷ [2]	"centralWidget"	QWidget
▲ [methods]	<3 items>	
showContextMenu		
showPreference		
updateTime		
▲ [parent]	@0x28fe24	QWidget
▷ [QObject]	@0x28fe24	QObject
▷ [QPaintDevice]	@0x28fe2c	QPaintDevice
▷ [children]	<1 items>	QObjectList
▷ [methods]	<27 items>	
[parent]	0x0	QObject *
▷ [properties]	<more than 0 items>	
▷ [signals]	<4 items>	
▷ data	@0x139a1f40	QWidgetData
▷ staticMetaObject	@0x9490068	QMetaObject
▷ [properties]	<more than 0 items>	
[signals]	<0 items>	
▷ m_mousePos	(0, 0)	QPoint
▷ staticMetaObject	@0x407004	QMetaObject
ui	@0x139a1830	Ui::MainWindow

As you can see from preceding screenshot, this is a `MainWindow` instance, which is inherited from `QMainWindow`. It has three children items: `_layout`, `qt_rubberband`, and `centralWidget`. It's noted that only slot functions are displayed in `[methods]`. Now you'll understand why the **Locals** pane is the most important and commonly used view in the **Debug** mode.

On the other hand, the **Expressions** pane is even more powerful and can compute the values of arithmetic expressions or function calls. Right-click on the **Locals and Expressions** view and select **Add New Expression Evaluator...** in the context menu.

Note that the context menu entries are available only when the program is interrupted. In this case, `Fancy_Clock` is interrupted in the `MainWindow::setColour()` function where the local variable, `i`, can be used to perform some arithmetic operations. For example, we fill `i * 5` in the **New Evaluated Expression** pop-up dialog.

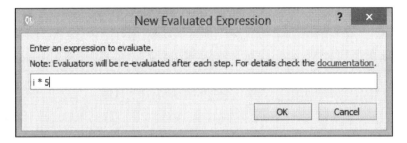

In addition to arithmetic operations, you can call a function to evaluate the return value. However, this function must be accessible to the debugger, which means it's either compiled into the executable or can be invoked from a library.

The expression value will be re-evaluated after each step. After you click on the **OK** button, the expression `i * 5`, is shown in the **Expressions** pane as shown here:

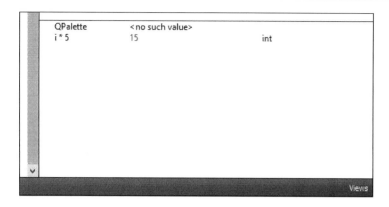

The value of i is now 3. Therefore, the expression i * 5 is evaluated as 15.

> *"Expression evaluators are powerful, but slow down debugger operation significantly. It is advisable not to use them excessively, and to remove unneeded expression evaluators as soon as possible."*

Even if functions used in the expressions have side effects, they will be called each time the current frame changes. After all, the expression evaluator is powerful but bad for debugging speed.

Debugging Qt Quick applications

We will use the Weather_QML project from *Chapter 7, Parsing JSON and XML Documents to Use Online APIs*, as a demonstration program to show how to debug a Qt Quick application.

First, we need to ensure that QML debugging is enabled. Open the Weather_QML project in Qt Creator. Then, perform the following steps:

1. Switch to the **Projects** mode.
2. Expand the **qmake** step in **Build Steps**.
3. Check **Enable QML debugging** if it's not checked.

> Debugging QML will open a socket at a well-known port, which poses a security risk. Anyone on your network could connect to the debugging application and execute any JavaScript function. Therefore, you have to make sure there are appropriate firewall rules.

The same procedure is used to start QML debugging, which is to navigate to **Debug | Start Debugging | Start Debugging**, or click the **Debug** button, or just press *F5*. It may trigger a **Windows Security Alert**, shown in the following screenshot. Don't forget to click on the **Allow access** button.

Once the application starts running, it behaves and performs as usual. However, you can perform some useful tasks in debugging mode. You can see all the elements and their properties in the **Locals** pane as we did for the Qt/C++ applications.

In addition to just watching these variables, you can change them temporarily and see the changes at runtime immediately. To change a value, you can either directly change it in the **Locals** pane or change it in **QML/JS Console**.

For example, to change the `title` property of `ApplicationWindow`, perform the following steps:

1. Expand **ApplicationWindow | Properties** in the **Locals** pane.
2. Double-click on the `title` entry.

3. Change the value from Weather QML to Yahoo! Weather.

4. Press the *Enter* or *Return* key on the keyboard to confirm.

Alternatively, you can change it in **QML/JS Console**. There is no need to expand
ApplicationWindow; just click on ApplicationWindow in the **Locals** pane. You'll
notice **Context** on the **QML/JS Console** panel will become ApplicationWindow, as
shown in the following screenshot. Then, just input the title="Yahoo! Weather"
command to change the title.

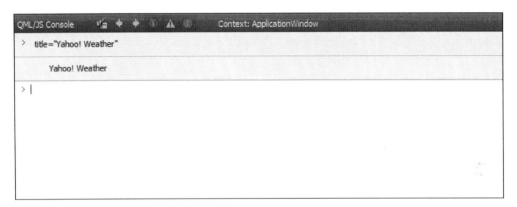

You'll notice the title in the application window is changed to **Yahoo! Weather**
immediately, as shown here:

Meanwhile, the source code is left intact. This feature is really handy when you want to test a better value for a property. Instead of changing it in the code and rerunning, you can change and test it on the fly. In fact, you can also execute the JavaScript expressions in **QML/JS Console**, not just change their values.

Useful resources

Still getting stuck with an issue? In addition to online search engines, there are two online forums that could also be useful for you. The first one is the forum in the Qt Project, whose URL is `http://qt-project.org/forums`. The other one is maintained by a community site, Qt Centre, and its URL is `http://www.qtcentre.org/forum.php`.

In most cases, you should be able to find similar or even identical problems on these websites. If not, you can post a new thread asking for help. Describe the problem as thoroughly as possible so that other users can get an idea of what's going wrong.

There is a possibility that you did everything correctly but still might be getting unexpected results, compiler errors, or crashes. In this case, it may be a Qt bug. If you believe that you've encountered a Qt bug, you are encouraged to report it. It's easy to report a bug since Qt has a bug tracker, whose URL is `https://bugreports.qt.io`.

 The quality of the bug report dramatically impacts how soon the bug will be fixed.

To produce a high-quality bug report, here is a simple step-by-step manual:

1. Visit the Qt bug tracker website.
2. Log in. If it's your first time, you need to create a new account. Remember to supply a valid e-mail address as this is the only way for the Qt developers to contact you.
3. Use the **Search** field on the upper-right side to find any similar, or even identical bugs.
4. If you find one, you can leave a comment with any additional information that you have. Besides, you can click on **Vote** to vote for that bug. Lastly, you could add yourself as a watcher if you want to track the progress.
5. If not, click on **Create New Issues** and fill in the fields.

You should enter a brief descriptive text in **Summary**. This is not only for a higher chance to get it fixed, but also good for other people searching for existing bugs. For other fields, you're always encouraged to provide as much information as you can.

Summary

After having a read through this chapter, you can sort out the majority of Qt-based issues on your own. We started off with a few commonly encountered problems, followed by how to debug Qt and Qt Quick applications. At the end, there were a few useful links to help you crack down on the varied issues and errors. If you encounter any problem with a particular Qt bug, don't panic, just go to the bug tracker and report it.

Index

Q

setValue function 38
show function 30
signals
  connecting 16
  using 7-15
slice function 101
slots
  about 8
  using 7-15
Stand-alone license paragraph 223
static linking
  versus dynamic linking 210
static plugins
  writing 113-121
status bar
  errors, displaying 88, 89
  permanent widgets 90-92
system network session
  managing 150-158

T

Thumbnail Toolbar 48
tr() function 192

U

Ubuntu 218
Unix platforms
  code, building 47-49
updateData function 168

V

Visual C++ Redistributable Packages 211

W

Where On Earth ID (WOEID) 166
widget layout
  modifying 6
windowFlags function 30
Windows
  Qt application, releasing 209-213
Windows Driver Kit (WDK)
  URL 237

X

XmlListModel
  used, for parsing RSS Feeds 57-63
XML
  results, parsing 177-182
  tutorial, URL 182

Y

Yahoo!
  Weather API, URL 165
  WOEID Lookup, URL 166

Thank you for buying
Qt 5 Blueprints

About Packt Publishing

Packt, pronounced 'packed', published its first book, *Mastering phpMyAdmin for Effective MySQL Management*, in April 2004, and subsequently continued to specialize in publishing highly focused books on specific technologies and solutions.

Our books and publications share the experiences of your fellow IT professionals in adapting and customizing today's systems, applications, and frameworks. Our solution-based books give you the knowledge and power to customize the software and technologies you're using to get the job done. Packt books are more specific and less general than the IT books you have seen in the past. Our unique business model allows us to bring you more focused information, giving you more of what you need to know, and less of what you don't.

Packt is a modern yet unique publishing company that focuses on producing quality, cutting-edge books for communities of developers, administrators, and newbies alike. For more information, please visit our website at www.packtpub.com.

About Packt Open Source

In 2010, Packt launched two new brands, Packt Open Source and Packt Enterprise, in order to continue its focus on specialization. This book is part of the Packt Open Source brand, home to books published on software built around open source licenses, and offering information to anybody from advanced developers to budding web designers. The Open Source brand also runs Packt's Open Source Royalty Scheme, by which Packt gives a royalty to each open source project about whose software a book is sold.

Writing for Packt

We welcome all inquiries from people who are interested in authoring. Book proposals should be sent to author@packtpub.com. If your book idea is still at an early stage and you would like to discuss it first before writing a formal book proposal, then please contact us; one of our commissioning editors will get in touch with you.

We're not just looking for published authors; if you have strong technical skills but no writing experience, our experienced editors can help you develop a writing career, or simply get some additional reward for your expertise.

Application Development with Qt Creator
Second Edition

ISBN: 978-1-78439-867-5   Paperback: 264 pages

Design and build dazzling cross-platform applications using Qt and Qt Quick

1. Imbibe the essential concepts of C++ and Qt Quick programming using Qt.

2. Write cross-platform mobile applications with Qt Creator.

3. Explore the core functions of Qt Creator using this step-by-step guide.

C++ Multithreading Cookbook

ISBN: 978-1-78328-979-0   Paperback: 422 pages

Over 60 recipes to help you create ultra-fast multithreaded applications using C++ with rules, guidelines, and best practices

1. Create multithreaded applications using the power of C++.

2. Upgrade your applications with parallel execution in easy-to-understand steps.

3. Stay up to date with new Windows 8 concurrent tasks.

4. Avoid classical synchronization problems.

Please check **www.PacktPub.com** for information on our titles

Learning Xamarin Studio

ISBN: 978-1-78355-081-4   Paperback: 248 pages

Learn how to build high-performance native applications using the power of Xamarin Studio

1. Get a full introduction to the key features and components of the Xamarin 3 IDE and framework, including Xamarin.Forms and iOS visual designer.

2. Install, integrate and utilise Xamarin Studio with the tools required for building amazing cross-platform applications for iOS and Android.

3. Create, test, and deploy apps for your business and for the app store.

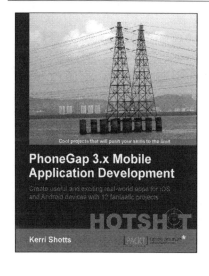

PhoneGap 3.x Mobile Application Development HOTSHOT

ISBN: 978-1-78328-792-5   Paperback: 450 pages

Create useful and exciting real-world apps for iOS and Android devices with 12 fantastic projects

1. Use PhoneGap 3.x effectively to build real, functional mobile apps ranging from productivity apps to a simple arcade game.

2. Explore often-used design patterns in apps designed for mobile devices.

3. Fully practical, project-based approach to give you the confidence in developing your app independently.

Please check **www.PacktPub.com** for information on our titles

Printed in Great Britain
by Amazon